Davy Crockett

Legends of the Wild West

Sitting Bull

Billy the Kid

Calamity Jane

Buffalo Bill Cody

Crazy Horse

Davy Crockett

Wyatt Earp

Geronimo

Wild Bill Hickok

Jesse James

Nat Love

Annie Oakley

Legends of the Wild West

Davy Crockett

Judy L. Hasday

CHELSEA HOUSE
PUBLISHERS
An imprint of Infobase Publishing

Davy Crockett

Copyright © 2010 by Infobase Publishing

Chelsea House
An imprint of Infobase Publishing
132 West 31st Street
New York NY 10001

Library of Congress Cataloging-in-Publication Data
Hasday, Judy L., 1957-
  Davy Crockett / Judy L. Hasday.
    p. cm. — (Legends of the wild West)
  Includes bibliographical references and index.
  ISBN 978-1-60413-592-3 (hardcover)
  1. Crockett, Davy, 1786-1836—Juvenile literature. 2. Pioneers—Tennessee
—Biography—Juvenile literature. 3. Frontier and pioneer life—Tennessee—Juvenile
literature. 4. Tennessee—Biography—Juvenile literature. 5. Legislators—United
States—Biography—Juvenile literature. 6. United States. Congress. House—
Biography—Juvenile literature. I. Title. II. Series.
  F436.C95H375 2010
  976.8'04092—dc22
  [B]   2009039442

Chelsea House books are available at special discounts when purchased in bulk quantities for businesses, associations, institutions, or sales promotions. Please call our Special Sales Department in New York at (212) 967-8800 or (800) 322-8755.

You can find Chelsea House on the World Wide Web at
http://www.chelseahouse.com

Text design by Kerry Casey
Cover design by Keith Trego
Composition by EJB Publishing Services
Cover printed by Bang Printing, Brainerd, Minn.
Book printed and bound by Bang Printing, Brainerd, Minn.
Date printed: December 2010
Printed in the United States of America

10 9 8 7 6 5 4 3 2

This book is printed on acid-free paper.

CONTENTS

CHILD OF
THE FRONTIER

Made a larger-than-life folk hero through stories of his adventures as a frontiersman, hunter, and militiaman, Davy Crockett may be most remembered for his heroic stand against the Mexican army at the Alamo on March 6, 1836. Born in a simple cabin along the banks of the Nolichucky River in Greene County, North Carolina, on August 17, 1786, David Stern Crockett was the fifth of nine children living in the small, cramped cabin that his father, John, had built for his wife, Rebecca, and his growing family. Named for his grandfather David who had come to America from Ireland, Davy Crockett was like many Americans whose family roots originated in Europe.

The Crocketts were descended from a captain in the Royal Guard of the king of France, Monsieur de la Croquetagne (or Crocketagne). In the seventeenth century, Croquetagne or his descendants, who were Huguenots (members of the Protestant Reformed Church of France who criticized the Roman Catholic Church) eventually fled France and settled in England and Ireland. Like millions of other immigrants, the Crocketts traveled across the vast waters of the Atlantic Ocean, hoping to find a better life in the newly founded country. Much of America was still very primitive, with vast expanses of the country yet to be developed. The wide-open territory was particularly appealing to those who wanted to go beyond the comforts and safety of existing towns to lay claim to the acres of open land on which to establish farms and ranches.

In America, David and his family continued to migrate, traveling from Maryland to Virginia, North Carolina, Tennessee, and Texas. The Crocketts settled in the Watauga area in East Tennessee, which was still part of North Carolina at the time. The Crocketts and some Watauga settlers had boldly chosen to put their stake on land that was not safe or welcoming to newcomers. Aside from the competition with other would-be settlers, David had to contend with unfriendly Native Americans. He had chosen to settle his homestead on lands allocated by treaty to the Creek and Cherokee nations. Watching their tribal lands being overrun by strangers greatly agitated the Native Americans. Davy, in his 1834 autobiography, *A Narrative of the Life of David Crockett of the State of Tennessee,* remarked about his grandfather's decision, saying, "He settled there under dangerous circumstances, both to himself and his family, as the country was full of Indians, who were at that time very troublesome."

The Native Americans became hostile, often attacking settlers whenever they came upon them. On a deadly day in 1777, a group of Creek came upon the Crockett homestead and attacked with a swiftness and surprise that gave those at home no chance to defend themselves. The oldest Crockett sons, John, William, and Robert, were away fighting with the Revolutionary army when David, his wife, Elizabeth, and about a dozen settlers were murdered. The two youngest Crockett boys, James and Joseph (who lost his arm in the massacre), were abducted, and one daughter was scalped but survived. Joseph and James lived with the Native Americans for the next 20 years.

SON OF A PIONEER

John, who would become Davy's father, served under Colonel Isaac Shelby in the Battle of Kings Mountain during the American

Revolutionary War (1775–1783). John was a member of a band of musket-toting settlers known as the "Over-mountain Men," a group of militiamen that defeated British major Robert Ferguson and his more than 1,100 troops. Historians consider the Battle of Kings Mountain, which was fought on October 7, 1780, to be a turning point in the war campaign in the South, as the British lost control of the Carolinas and had to give up hopes of marching north into Virginia. Just a little more than a year later, Patriot general George Washington accepted the surrender of British general Charles Cornwallis at Yorktown, Virginia, effectively ending the war.

John married Rebecca Hawkins in 1780. According to Davy Crockett in his autobiography, Hawkins had come from Maryland to Holston Valley, Tennessee, with her father, Nathan, and her mother, Ruth. The valley was just south of the Virginia border. No details were recorded about his future parents' courtship other than their marriage.

When John returned from the war, he became a commissioner for building roads, and in 1783, a frontier ranger. John and his growing family lived on Limestone Creek in Greene County, North Carolina, when their fifth child, Davy, was born in 1786. A few years later, they moved to nearby Cove Creek. John worked hard, wanting to make a prosperous life for Rebecca and their children; unfortunately, he was often in debt and involved in failed business ventures. One such venture, building a gristmill with a partner, Thomas Galbraith, literally washed away. Overtaken by a flash flood, the mill was broken up by the strength of the rushing water and carried downstream. Fortunately, John was an excellent hunter, as his son Davy would one day be, and was able to at least provide food for the family while he figured out what to do next.

With the mill gone and the family in debt, the Crocketts moved to 300 acres (121 hectares) of land between Abingdon, Virginia, and Knoxville, Tennessee, in Jefferson County (now Hamblen County). The property sat along the main wagon route between the two towns, so John built a roadside tavern that could accommodate his family

Born on August 17, 1786, in what is now Greene County, Tennessee, Davy Crockett was the fifth of nine children in a family that experienced hardship and adventure. A replica of the cabin where he was born stands at the Davy Crockett Birthplace Historic Site in Limestone, Tennessee.

and any travelers seeking a room for the night. It was a difficult existence for the Crocketts. Davy would later recall in *Narrative*:

> His tavern was on a small scale, as he was poor; and the principal accommodations which he kept, were for the Avaggoners [wagoners, or travelers] who travelled the road. Here I remained with him until I was twelve years old; and about that time, you may guess, if you belong to Yankee land, or reckon, if like me you belong to the back-woods, that I began to make up my acquaintance with hard times, and a plenty of them.

BOUND OUT FOR SERVICE

Even as a young boy, Davy recognized his father's plight. Though the tavern did have customers, it was not earning enough money for John to pay the $400 debt on the 300 acres he bought on which to build it. The county sheriff had no choice but to seize the property. Forced to sell his land at a public auction, John received a negligible $40 from the new owner, William Line. Out of sympathy or lack of interest, Line allowed John to keep the tavern. Despite being able to stay and run the business, John needed another way to make money to take care of the family. With no other options, he was forced to hire out his young son Davy. The practice was known as "bound boys." When cattle driver Jacob Siler stopped at the tavern on his way to Virginia with a herd, he struck a deal with John to pay Davy a small fee to help him take the cattle the rest of the 200-mile (322-kilometer) journey north.

Scared, homesick, and traveling with a bunch of strangers, the obedient 12-year-old knew he had no choice but to work for Mr. Siler. The trip north was cold and miserable. Davy often walked through snowdrifts, bracing himself against the high winds that made each step heavier and more exhausting. It took two weeks to get to their destination. Davy was tired and sad but knew he had been bound by his duty to his father to fulfill his agreement with Siler. Once the cattle were delivered, however, Siler was reluctant to let Davy return home. He tried to bribe him by paying him extra money, but soon the youngster was working on a way to leave unnoticed. As luck would have it, one day a band of wagoners passed through town. Davy approached one of the men, whom he recognized from his father's tavern named Dunn. Mr. Dunn agreed to help him and met up with Davy the next morning away from the Siler home.

It took Davy many days to make his way back home, accepting the help of people along the way before he finally left to walk the last 15 miles (24 km) or so back to the tavern. He was glad to be home with his family again, but he remained for only about one year before he would again have to leave. After his return from his trek to Virginia, Davy and his brothers began to attend school to learn the basics of reading, writing, and arithmetic. Davy never really liked school and did not always get along with the other students. A run-in with an older boy left Davy angry and wanting revenge. He jumped the boy as he walked along the road after school, inflicting several cuts and bruises. Feelings of revenge quickly turned to panic when Davy realized he would probably be punished for fighting when he returned to school. Avoiding the wrath of the schoolmaster, Davy stayed away from class for several days. Finally, a note was sent home inquiring about Davy's absences. John was furious and chased Davy until he could no longer see him in his sights.

RUNAWAY

The next morning Davy ran away from home. He remembered that his brother had signed on to work with a neighbor, Jesse Cheek, who was moving a herd of cattle. Cheek was happy to give Davy a job, too; so for the second time in a little more than a year, he would be working on another long cattle drive. The destination was Fort Royal, nearly 400 miles (644 km) from the family tavern in Tennessee. When the cattle were delivered, Davy started to head back home but found his fear of his father's anger and the schoolmaster's punishment reason enough to stay away. Instead, over the next few years, Davy's home became the frontier, where he grew from a young teen into a skilled and self-sufficient man. Author Buddy Levy states in *American Legend: The Real Life Adventures of Davy Crockett*, "Davy relied on his guile and savvy to survive alone, living from one adventure to the next. . . . To survive the rigors of the road, a young boy needed to be smart, industrious, resilient, and something of an actor, and all these traits—plus others like ambition and pride—began to germinate in the youngster."

Davy had many jobs during his time away, earning money wherever he could. He worked for a while as a farmhand and for a hatter named Elijah Griffith. He originally signed on for four years, but after 18 months, Griffith's business went bust and Davy was once

Life on the frontier was difficult, and pioneer families needed to be self-sufficient in order to survive. Crockett would learn how to hunt and trap game using a rifle and would become an expert marksman, skills that would help him become the American folk hero whose life is celebrated today.

again without work or money. He had traveled much of the territory from Tennessee to Baltimore, Maryland, always trying to work his way south back to the tavern and his family. He had survived the harsh conditions of the open road, plodding through snow, canoeing down a swift and cold river, getting soaked to the bone in the process, and walking miles upon miles until he found a place to rest and earn his next dollar to buy food and shelter.

When he lost his job with the hatter, Davy decided it was time to make his way home. He arrived at the tavern late one evening, concealing his identity. When he left he was a 13-year-old boy; now he returned almost 16 years of age and had grown and filled out more to a man's build and size. He asked for a room for the night and stayed off to the side until everyone gathered at the supper table. It was Davy's oldest sister who recognized him first, jumping up from the table in delight to hug her long-lost brother. Davy felt instantly at ease, sorry that he had worried about what kind of welcome he would receive. In *Narrative*, Davy wrote:

> My feelings at this time it would be vain and foolish for me to attempt to describe. I had often thought I felt before, and I suppose I had, but sure I am, I never had felt as I then did. The joy of my sisters and my mother, and, indeed, of all the family, was such that it humbled me, and made me sorry that I hadn't submitted to a hundred whippings, sooner than cause so much affliction as they had suffered on my account.

THE DUTIFUL SON

After enjoying the excitement of his return, Davy learned of the life his family had led in his absence. His father continued to struggle financially, acquiring more creditors and debt. John realized that his son's return home might help with the debt. The two came to an agreement: Davy would help him settle a few of the debts and then would be free of his obligation to his father. There was one debt in particular that was most worrisome to John, a $36 (about $600 today) debt to a man named Abraham Wilson. Davy agreed to work for Wilson to settle the debt. For the next six months, he worked tirelessly for Wilson, not missing one day's labor. When the debt was paid in what Davy would have earned in wages, Wilson offered to keep him on as a hired hand. Davy politely declined, for he did not think much of Wilson's business. In *Narrative*, Davy wrote,

> When my time was out, I got my father's note, and then declined working with the man any longer, though he wanted to hire me mighty bad. The reason was, it was a place where a heap of bad company met to drink and gamble, and I wanted to get away from them, for I know'd [sic] very well if I staid [sic] there, I should get a bad name, as nobody could be respectable that would live there.

After leaving Wilson's "employ," Davy went to work for a Quaker farmer named John Kennedy to take care of another of his father's debts. John Crockett owed Kennedy $40. When Davy worked off the debt, he took the note to his father intending to show him that it, too, was paid. Initially, John thought his son was bringing him another unpaid note. Davy reassured his father that the debt to Kennedy was also paid. John Crockett, overcome with gratitude, "shed a heap of tears" and told his son he was too poor to give him anything in return. Davy asked only to be free to start building his own life. John understood his young son was now a man and needed to be free of his family responsibilities. Davy left his father's home for the last time and headed back to the Kennedy farm. He was going to work now to earn his own money, something entirely new to him.

COURTIN' AND MARRIAGE

Never having had his own money before, except to get ways to travel home from one situation or another, Davy Crockett looked forward to earning money so that he could begin to buy some of the things he needed and had not been able to afford up until now. He had worked almost a full year settling his father's debts and had not earned a penny for himself. His clothes were old and worn out from the many labors he had undertaken. Wanting to be regarded as a respectable man, despite his limited education, Crockett knew he needed to make changes in his appearance if he was going to have any chance of finding and courting a proper wife.

Working on Kennedy's farm was uneventful for Crockett until he had been there about two months. Kennedy's niece came for a visit from North Carolina, and as soon as Crockett laid eyes on her he was love-struck. It took him a while before he got up the courage to speak to her. Crockett had not had much experience in the ways of romance and love and felt if he tried to talk to the girl all that would come out of his mouth would be a jumble of words. In *Narrative*, Crockett wrote about his struggle, saying,

In the early nineteenth century, poor children like Davy Crockett were able to attend school only when they were not working on the family farm. Therefore, children were able to attend school for limited amounts of time, in a single classroom with other students that ranged from 4 to 21. In this picture, children of various ages stand in front of a one-room sod schoolhouse in Kansas Territory.

> I soon found myself head over heels in love with this girl, whose name the public could make no use of . . . but I was afraid to begin, for when I would think of saying anything to her, my heart would begin to flutter like a duck in a puddle; and if I tried to outdo it and speak, it would get right smack up in my throat, and choak me like a cold potatoe.

He should not have worried. When he finally got up the nerve to talk to her, she was kind and flattered. But she was also engaged to one of the Kennedy sons and therefore unavailable to court.

Crockett was devastated like any young man would be over a love's rejection, but he also felt he had no chance with this girl because he was not well schooled. When Crockett was a boy, he had not taken book learning too seriously, but now he felt it was important.

Crockett learned that one of Kennedy's sons was a school-teacher who lived about a mile and a half (2.5 km) from the elder Kennedy's homestead. He was running a small school, and Crockett thought it would be a good idea to attend. With little money to pay the younger Kennedy for his teaching, Crockett made a deal with him. He had already learned how to trade off his labor in exchange for settling debts. Why not offer to work in exchange for being taught how to read and write? Kennedy was agreeable. Crockett would come to class four days a week and work for him two other days to pay for his board and schooling. Crockett went about his lessons with the same intensity as he had everything else he put his mind to. He followed the schedule for about six months, learning to write his own name, read in his primer, and master some basic arithmetic skills.

IN SEARCH OF A WIFE

Six months was about all the schooling Crockett could take. Aside from his early days attending school before he ran away, this was all the formal education Crockett would receive in his lifetime. He figured he could continue his learning on his own now that he had the basics understood. At 18, Crockett had some of the "book learned" skills and enough of the practical knowledge on survival to take care of himself. He was too impatient to find a wife to divide his time with classroom studies, and as Crockett is so aptly quoted in *American Legend*, "I couldn't do any longer without a wife; and so I cut out to hunt me one."

Crockett discovered rather quickly that finding a wife would not be that easy. Partnering with a woman was not as simple as agreeing to work off a debt. Nor was it as simple as just taking a fancy to a woman and having her agreeable to the arrangement of marriage. It may have been a frustrating and, at times, painful process, but when

Crockett remembered how elated he was after he had fallen head over heels in love with Kennedy's niece, it only fueled his quest that much more. The real challenge was in figuring out where to search for eligible women. Crockett thought about it for a while and then remembered a family from his youth. There were three attractive daughters in the Elder family, and Crockett thought that any one of them would make a suitable bride.

When he paid a visit to the Elder home, Crockett found himself attracted to daughter Margaret. He made his interest in her very clear and asked if she might permit him to court her. Margaret agreed. Some accounts of Margaret Elder portray her as flirtatious but shy. Crockett's feelings for Margaret deepened quickly, just as they had for John Kennedy's niece. He pressed her often about marriage, but she remained unwilling to make a commitment. By the time Crockett escorted her to the Kennedy niece's wedding, he was ready to explode from all the waiting for Margaret to say yes. Crockett again found himself worked up and suffering from the fever that being in love brings. Wrote Crockett in *Narrative*, "I would have agreed to fight a whole regiment of wild cats if she would only have said she would have me."

DECEIVED AGAIN

Crockett continued to pressure Margaret about marriage until she finally broke down and consented. They set a wedding date and Crockett thought he was now the happiest man in the world. Things were looking promising for the first time for as long as he could remember. He had bought a new rifle that he took with him everywhere, including shooting matches he had begun to enter for quarters of beef. He had become an expert marksman and thought he was good enough to perhaps win a few of those matches. Though Crockett may have overestimated his fortunes with women, he was right about his shooting skills. Just a few days before he and Margaret were to be wed, he stopped by one of those matches and, with a partner, won a whole beef. Crockett sold his half of the beef for five dollars and, with money in his pocket and a contented feeling in his heart, he headed over to see his gal.

On his way to the Elder home, Crockett stopped by the house of one of Margaret's uncles. As Crockett had not officially asked for Margaret's hand in marriage, he was a little nervous about how her parents would react to the news. Thinking he might get some insight from the uncle on how to proceed, Crockett went in the house to engage in some chit-chat. To his surprise, one of Margaret's sisters was already in the house. Crockett felt a sudden tension in the room. Looking horrified by Crockett's presence, the sister burst into tears. She blurted out that Margaret had cruelly deceived Crockett, for she was to wed another man the very next day. Crockett described what those words made him feel in his autobiography:

> This was as sudden to me as a clap of thunder of a bright sunshiny day. It was the cap-stone of all the afflictions I had ever met with; and it seemed to me, that it was more than any human creature could endure. It struck me perfectly speechless for some time, and made me feel so weak, that I thought I should sink down.

Despite her decree as to Margaret's intentions, her sister tried to convince Crockett to fight for her hand in marriage. She told him that even though he had not asked for their permission, her mother and father preferred Crockett as a son-in-law. Nevertheless, he was too stunned, too shocked, and too crushed to do anything but head out the door and go back to his room at the Kennedy home.

Dejected and believing that he was to live his life enduring one disappointment after another and destined to be forever without a partner, Crockett fell into a deep depression. To ease his pain, he did what he did best—hunt. It took his mind off his troubles and his feelings of failure, and it gave him something pleasurable to do to break up the otherwise routine existence of long, backbreaking days working.

On one of his evening excursions, Crockett came upon the home of a widow and her daughter. He had known them to nod and say a polite hello, but was not otherwise interested in them. That day, however, they got to talking, and Crockett blurted out his woes and misfortune. To cheer him up, they invited him to their family's "reaping"—a celebratory party that could last several days—where he was promised an introduction to one of the prettiest girls he had ever laid eyes upon. Reapings were also opportunities for men to be in a more relaxed social setting to meet women. Crockett accepted the invitation and actually looked forward to the event. The two women had piqued his curiosity and, though skeptical, he wanted to see who this girl was that they had picked out for him.

GOOD FORTUNE AT LAST

Her name was Mary "Polly" Finley, a pretty Irish lass who did not disappoint Crockett when he first gazed upon her. They talked for a while, and once the party got into full swing, they danced together. Night turned into morning, and Crockett felt he had never had such an enjoyable time. He decided that Miss Polly Finley was worth courting and, as not to make the same mistake again, he would court her mother, Jean Kennedy Finley, too. What Crockett did not know until his first calling on Polly was that he had competition. Another suitor was vying for Polly's hand in marriage. At least this time it was all out in the open. Crockett never backed away from a challenge, and he was determined to win this one.

The courtship was not a long one. After earning enough money to buy a second horse, the one his new bride would ride off on, Crockett went to the Finleys' home so he and Polly could set the date to be married. For some reason, Jean flew into a hollering rage and ordered Crockett out of the house. Still, Polly happily agreed to be with Crockett, and she promised to leave with him when he arrived the following Thursday to pick her up and head off to their wedding. Taking no chances, Crockett secured a marriage license and, as per custom in those days, assembled an entourage to go with him to the Finleys'.

On Thursday, August 14, 1806, Crockett saddled up along with his eldest brother and his wife, another brother, one of his sisters,

On the frontier, a wedding celebration would take place over several days, with the whole community taking part. Like most brides and grooms, Crockett probably wore a handed-down suit and his bride wore a dress of calico. Those attending would wear the finest clothes they owned—like this Kentucky wedding party shown above in 1800—and would enjoy games, singing, dancing, and a great amount of food.

and two fellow friends, and rode off to the Finley house. About two miles (3 km) from their destination, the Crockett party was met by a large group that seemed to be waiting for them. Crockett knew that this was part of the marriage custom. He had brought with him an empty flagon— a large metal or pottery jug used to hold beverages like wine—and he sent it off with his best man to give to the folks in waiting. If the flagon returned filled with liquor, it meant Crockett had William Finley's consent to marry his daughter. A considerable time later, his friend galloped back with the flagon so full it was spilling over the rim. Permission received, Crockett and his group trotted up to the house to collect his bride-to-be.

After some additional bickering between Crockett and Jean, she agreed to the marriage. Since Polly was her first child to be wed, she wanted the event to be special and would do whatever she could to make that happen if Crockett agreed to hold the wedding at their house instead of going off to a justice of the peace. Not wanting any more problems or delays, Crockett gave in, and he and his bride were married two days later on August 16, 1806. It was just one day shy of Crockett's twentieth birthday. Polly's dowry was meager, but it was generous based on the Finleys' financial circumstances. They gave the newlyweds two cows with their calves, and Crockett rented a farm with a cabin near Polly's parents on Bay Mountain, Tennessee. He hoped to work the land and make a home for himself and Polly. Old friend John Kennedy gave the couple a gift order for $15 worth of things they could use to set up a home in the rented cabin.

Initially, Crockett thought he had everything he wanted. But after the excitement of the wedding had subsided, he wrote in *Narrative*:

> . . . having gotten my wife, I thought I was completely made up, and needed nothing more in the whole world. But I soon found this was all a mistake—for now having a wife, I wanted everything else; and, worse than all, I had nothing to give for it.

The reality was that Davy Crockett was rich in his heart but poor in his pockets. He knew that lots of hard work and struggle awaited him.

LIFE ON THE FRONTIER

Like many sharecroppers of the time, Crockett found that renting and cultivating farmland to grow crops was exhausting, sometimes backbreaking, work and not very profitable. He was paying more in rent for being on the farm than the land's harvests were yielding in dollars. Said Crockett in *Narrative*: "We worked on for some years, renting ground, and paying high rent, until I found it wan't [sic] the thing it was cracked up to be; and that I couldn't make a fortune at it just at all."

Many families living on the frontier often found where they settled to be unproductive. It became common practice to just pack up your belongings and move farther west, even if it was only just a few miles away from where you had been. Out on the frontier, there was always the hope that things might be better down the road. Crockett got to the point where he felt he had to do just that. Though he could hunt and put food on the table, he could not make enough money to pay for the other things a family needed. The Crocketts had grown to four in their time at Bay Mountain. Polly had given birth to a son, John Wesley, on July 10, 1807. Two years later, on November 25, 1809, a second son, William, was born. Crockett noted in his autobiography that he had been more

Farming during Crockett's time was extremely hard work, and nearly all of it was done by hand. The main crops were corn, wheat, rye, barley, and oats, and the food reaped during the harvesting season had to last throughout the rest of the year. The pioneers shown are planting corn on nearly cleared land in the backwoods.

successful at increasing his family than at increasing his wealth. He had yet to realize, however, that he just was not cut out for plowing land; his calling was to be out in the wilderness hunting, tracking, scouting, and fighting wars.

With William Finley's help, Crockett moved the family about 150 miles (241 km) west to a much smaller tract of land in Lincoln County near the Elk River. It was state land, and Crockett applied for title on the property as a homesteader. He built a new cabin for his family and even carved his initials into a nearby beech tree.

While he should have been spending the bulk of his time planting crops and building pens to corral the cattle, Crockett was more drawn to exploring the untouched land around his home. Wild game was plentiful, and Crockett found himself spending more time in the woods hunting than he did farming. It was during this time that Crockett also began to realize his great skill as a hunter, but he knew he had a farm to take care of. Polly had also given birth on November 25, 1812, to a daughter, whom they named Margaret. With an ever-increasing family, Crockett continued to try to make a go of it. He even put himself in debt by putting in a claim for 15 more acres (6 ha). Crockett thought more land might yield more crops and would earn more money.

Despite his toil and sweat, Crockett still was unable to pay the taxes on the additional land and eventually lost it all. For the second time in four years, the Crocketts were forced to move. Traveling by horse and wagon with the kids, horses, and his trusty guns, Crockett moved the family to Franklin County, settling along Bean's Creek, Tennessee, near the Alabama border. So focused on his own lot in life, Crockett was not keenly aware that he had become one of the men pushing to settle the western frontier. He was probably also unaware that these white settlers were encroaching on lands that they had no right to occupy. Treaties were made and then broken, and Native Americans were losing more and more of the land they had occupied long before the first white settlers appeared and were becoming more and more hostile toward their intruders. Sitting alongside Bean's Creek soaking in the tranquility of the wilderness, Crockett could not have imagined he would soon be using his hunting and marksman skills in war.

THE WAR OF 1812

Despite America's winning its independence from the British in 1783, there were many attacks upon the United States that continued to fuel ill feelings toward Great Britain. Two major issues were at the heart of the continued rift: the continuing seizure and sale of American merchant ships and their cargo under the pretext of violating the British blockade of Europe, and impressments (forced recruitment) of captured U.S. seamen into the Royal Navy. Britain was still battling with the French over control of the Northwest Territories and Canada. In reality, many in the States also wanted Britain out of Canada, having their own ideas about expanding the United States northward. Several Southern states—Georgia, Tennessee, and the Mississippi Territory—had designs on conquering Florida, which the British had returned to Spanish control at the end of the American Revolution.

By the third year into James Madison's presidency, British ships had captured almost 400 American ships. Some of those seizures occurred within view of the U.S. coast. Americans were feeling more and more like the Revolutionary War had not really ended. Wrote John Clopton of Virginia as documented in *Reliving History —The War of 1812: Causes*:

> The outrages in impressing American seamen exceed all manner of description. Indeed, the whole system of aggression now is such that the real question between Great Britain and the United States has ceased to be a question merely relating to certain rights of commerce . . . it is now clearly, positively, and directly a question of independence, that is to say, whether the United States are really an independent nation.

Madison (a former secretary of state who supervised the Louisiana Purchase, doubling the size of the United States) had tried many methods to end the aggression. He tried diplomacy and even nonmilitary force, imposing economic pressure against England to remove its blockade. The Non-Intercourse Act of 1807 was reinstated; it prohibited British and French ships from entering U.S. ports and declared it illegal for American citizens to have "any intercourse with, or to afford any aid or supplies" to any ships flying French or British colors. The embargo against the British coincided with a poor grain harvest in England and a more critical need for American exports to supply the British troops who were still engaged in war with France. Realizing the embargo was hurting his country, on June 16, 1812, British foreign minister Augustus J. Foster announced the blockade would end against American ships. Unfortunately Madison and the U.S. Congress, out of patience with the British and having not received Foster's announcement in time, voted to go to war on June 18, 1812.

War Brewing Farther South

The British found willing allies. There was no love lost between many of the Native Americans and the settlers. Incursions by white settlers throughout the frontier gave the Native Americans plenty of incentive to join up with the British to drive the Americans out of Canada. In Florida, the Spanish were supplying weapons and supplies to the Creek tribe living in the Gulf Coast territories. One faction of the Creek Nation, the Red Stick (known as such because they painted their war clubs red) were eager to take on the settlers overrunning their lands in Alabama and Georgia. Concerned about a major Creek uprising, U.S. cavalry colonel James Caller assembled 180 militiamen to find the Red Stick and seize the purchased munitions.

On July 27, 1813, the cavalry came upon a small band of Creek at Burnt Corn Creek, in Alabama. The cavalry ambushed the Creek, who scattered, leaving their possessions behind. Thinking they had just won a bloodless battle, the militiamen began going through the Creek's belongings. They did not know the Native Americans had regrouped. Led by Red Stick leader Peter McQueen, the Creek counterattacked, sending the militia scrambling. No one knows how many were wounded or died in what became known as the Battle of Burnt Corn, but two things were certain: the battle was a huge embarrassment to the soldiers, and this "skirmish" led to the Creek War (1813–1814).

The great Shawnee chief Tecumseh, who had endured and heard enough about the displacement, dishonored treaties, and illegal seizure of Native American lands, had railed against the white man more than a year before. In Robert Blaisdell's book,

Tecumseh: Respected Warrior and Leader of the Shawnee

In about 1768, the Shawnee were trying to reunite in the Ohio Valley, from which they had been displaced in the seventeenth century. They aimed to defend the territory against white expansion. The Shawnee eventually moved to the Maumee River, where they joined with other tribes to resist the white settlement of the Northwest. During these raids, Tecumseh, under the leadership of his oldest brother, Cheeseekau, distinguished himself as a brave and loyal warrior. As white settlers forced his tribe farther westward, he became enraged at their attempts to seize land and participated in several raids against them.

(continues)

A depiction of Tecumseh, leader of the Shawnee, in 1848.

(continued)

When Tecumseh became chief of the Shawnee, he, with his brother, Tenskwatawa, settled their people in Indiana near the confluence of the Wabash and Tippecanoe rivers, in what they called Prophetstown. Tecumseh proposed that the area tribes form a confederacy and refuse to give or sell land to whites unless all the tribes in the confederacy agreed. He convinced many villages to join in his resistance and gained followers who moved to Prophetstown. At the height of Tecumseh's influence, he may have had up to 5,000 warrior followers.

Tecumseh's confederacy gained support from the British settlers in Canada, who wanted to prevent the United States from expanding westward—but this did not sit well with the U.S. government. In 1810, the chief met with the governor of Indiana Territory, William H. Harrison (who would later become president of the United States), in what became known as the Council of Vincennes. Indiana Territory at the time included parts of present-day Indiana, Illinois, Wisconsin, and Michigan. Tecumseh delivered a passionate speech demanding that land-purchase treaties in the area between the tribes and the U.S. government be rescinded. The demand was not met, and the meeting was so quarrelsome that it almost became violent.

Spurred to greater action, Tecumseh traveled south in 1811 to meet with leaders of the Five Civilized Tribes—the Cherokee, Chickasaw, Choctaw, Creek, and Seminole. Tecumseh hoped to persuade them to join his confederacy. In Tecumseh's absence, Harrison led a preemptive attack against the Shawnee and their allies and destroyed Prophetstown.

After Tecumseh returned home, he began rebuilding the confederacy and established an alliance with the British in Canada. When war broke out between the United States and Great Britain in 1812, Tecumseh led several raids against American forces and helped the British capture Fort Detroit. In 1813, U.S. forces attacked Prophetstown again, destroying it for the second time before launching an invasion of Canada. Tecumseh helped cover the British retreat into Canada, but the U.S. forces, led by Harrison, now commander of the Army of the Northwest, were overwhelming. Tecumseh was killed during the Battle of the Thames on October 5, 1813.

Great Speeches by Native Americans, Tecumseh's words of rage still resonate:

> Muscogees, brethren of my mother, brush from your eyelids the sleep of slavery; once more strike for vengeance; once more for your country. The spirits of the mighty dead complain. Their tears drop from the weeping skies. Let the white race perish.
>
> They seize your land; they corrupt your women; they trample on the ashes of your dead!
>
> Back, whence they came, upon a trail of blood, they must be driven.
>
> Back! back, ay, into the great water whose accursed waves brought them to our shores!
>
> Burn their dwellings! Destroy their stock! Slay their wives and children! The Red Man owns the country, and the Pale-faces must never enjoy it.
>
> War now! War forever! War upon the living! War upon the dead! Dig their very corpses from the grave. Our country must give no rest to a white man's bones.

The Creek were ready for vengeance and their own surprise attack. The nearby settlers' safe haven, Fort Mims, was the target. Unaware and unprepared, the settlers, Mississippi militia, and the mixed-blood Creek inhabiting the fort were open prey for the Creek. Even the gates to the fort were somehow left open, giving the raging tribe uncontested access. Led by Chief Red Eagle, the Red Stick savagely attacked, killing and wounding hundreds of men, women, and children before setting the fort on fire. In his book, *Red Eagle and the Wars with the Creek Indians of Alabama,* George Cary Eggleston writes,

> The fighting was terrible. It was not two bodies of troops struggling for possession of some strategic point, but a horde of savages battling with a devoted band of white

Five hundred mixed-blood Creeks, Mississippi militia, and white settlers were killed during the attack at Fort Mims on August 30, 1813. What started as a civil war within the Creek tribe became a war between the United States and the Red Stick. Davy Crockett left his home and joined the volunteer militia to participate in what became the Creek War.

men in a struggle the only issue of which was death. The savages fought not to conquer but to kill the whites, every one, women and children as well as men; and the whites fought with the desperation of doomed men whose only chance of life was in victory. It was hand-to-hand fighting, too. It was fighting with knives and tomahawks and clubbed guns. Men grappled with each other, to relinquish their hold only in death.

The battle raged for several hours before those remaining were taken prisoner. It was a decisive victory for the Red Stick, but enraged American settlers knew war had come to the frontier.

BATTLING THE RED STICK

The shock of the attack against the people at Fort Mims quickly wore off and was replaced by anger and resolve to hunt out the Red Stick and defeat them. A call went out to all available men to join volunteer militias to help in the fight. Crockett was usually a man with a rather good-natured manner, more interested in hunting and making something of his latest homestead. When news of the Red Stick massacre reached him, however, he thought he should join the fight. He wrote in *Narrative*:

> The Creek Indians had commenced their open hostilities by a most bloody butchery at Fort [Mims]. There had been no war among us for so long . . . when I heard of the mischief which was done at the fort, I instantly felt like going, and I had none of the dread of dying that I expected to feel . . . my countrymen had been murdered, and I knew that the next thing would be, that the Indians would be scalping the women and children all about there, if we didn't put a stop to it.

When Crockett told Polly of his decision to join up with a militia, she begged him not to go. She did not want to be left in a strange new territory to parent the children alone. She asked him who would work the farm in his absence. How would they have food to eat and fuel to keep them warm? Crockett listened to his wife's concerns and pondered them, not sure how to answer her fears. Ultimately, he thought that if every man listened to his wife and stayed behind, there wouldn't be enough men to fight off the Native Americans, and eventually everyone would meet the same fate as those at Fort Mims.

To prepare for his departure, Crockett hunted as much wild game as he could to keep food on the table for Polly and the children. In turn, when it was time to leave, Polly packed up as much food as he could take with him and bid him a safe return. Crockett headed off to Winchester, Tennessee, where the other men in the area agreed to meet up. They wound up with a rather large company of volunteers, with Crockett himself signing up to serve for 60 days. Later, as he rode off with his company, he hoped this wouldn't be a long, drawn out war. He really just wanted to return to his family safely and get back to his life alongside Mulberry Creek, sitting quietly under the tree with his carved initials.

THE WOODSMAN GOES TO WAR

President Madison wanted to end the random, sporadic attacks by the Red Stick. He knew well of their inspirational leader, Shawnee chief Tecumseh, whose powerful oratory along with his brother Tenskwatawa's prophecy skills had managed to rouse the anger and resentment of Native Americans in the southern region of the United States. Fearing the wider-spread unity among tribes across the country that Tecumseh was trying to coordinate, the Madison administration put together a military response, assembling four armies and sending them into the core of the region occupied by the Creek Nation. Armies from Georgia, Tennessee, and the area known as the Mississippi Territory were to meet up where the Tallapoosa and Coosa rivers converged (about 10 miles, or 16 km, northeast of present-day Montgomery, Alabama). The administration's thinking was that the renegade Red Stick would not be able to withstand such a show of force.

Crockett's enlistment officially began on September 24, 1813. He was part of the 2nd Regiment of Volunteer Mounted Riflemen. The men came from many Tennessee counties, including Bedford, Rutherford, Smith, Dickson, Franklin, Lincoln, Sumner, Williamson, and Wilson. When Crockett went to Winchester to

On March 27, 1814, United States forces under the leadership of General Andrew Jackson (*above*) defeated the Red Stick, ending the Creek War. Davy Crockett served as a scout for Jackson during the Creek War.

volunteer, a lawyer named Francis Jones was forming the militia. The men who signed on, including Crockett, elected Jones captain of the regiment. Jones would later go on to serve as a Tennessee congressman. The men would fall under the immediate command of Colonel John Coffee, a frontier planter and good friend of General Andrew Jackson.

The 2nd Regiment rode out of Winchester and headed to its rendezvous point with the other units. It set up camp at Beaty's Spring, near Huntsville, Alabama, awaiting everyone else's arrival. Word began spreading around the ever-growing camp that General Andrew Jackson was assigned as the commander of the army from Tennessee. He and his foot soldiers were on their way from Nashville. Jackson had a well-established reputation as a hot head, but also as a fierce fighter in battle. Severely protective of his honor, he had killed a man in a duel back in 1806 and was wounded while trying to intervene in a duel between one of his officers and a man named Jesse Benton. Jackson was a shrewd man who had political aspirations and understood that gaining military glory was one of the ingredients to political advancement.

Fighting the Native Americans excited Jackson as he had developed strong disdain and prejudice for them as early as his teen years. He believed, as did many white settlers of the time, that the Native Americans were in the way of developing the frontier and should be removed to make way for expansion west. Crockett did not harbor such deep prejudices, despite the slaughter of his grandparents by Native American hands. He was, however, mindful of his patriotic duty, and that meant a great deal to him. Whatever the motivations of the men who joined in the cause, there was great excitement and even a sense of relief over the news that Jackson would lead them into battle.

AM I NOT QUALIFIED?

While the men waited for Jackson's arrival, Coffee's subordinate Major John H. Gibson requested to have two men go out with him on a scouting mission. The purpose of the expedition was to learn as much as possible about the Creek's battle plans. Gibson was specific about who should be recommended—excellent woodsmen who could handle a rifle well. Captain Jones immediately suggested Crockett, who was one of the best at finding his way around in the backwoods and was an expert shot with the rifle. Crockett agreed to go and asked if he could pick who would accompany them. Gibson agreed, but quickly regretted his decision when Crockett chose George Russell, a young man who was still more boy than a man. He was the son of a friend of Crockett's from Franklin County. Gibson scoffed, and as Crockett wrote in *Narrative*, he got annoyed over it:

> Gibson said he thought he hadn't beard enough to please him,—he wanted men, and not boys. I must confess I was a little nettled at this; for I know'd George Russell, and I know'd there was no mistake in him; and I didn't think that courage ought to be measured by the beard, for fear a goat would have the preference over a man. I told the major he was on the wrong scent; that Russell could go as far as he could, and I must have him along. He saw I was a little wrathy, and said I had the best chance of knowing, and agreed that it should be as I wanted it.

The following morning 13 men left the camp, including Gibson, Crockett, and Russell. They crossed the Tennessee River at Ditto's Landing in the northern part of Alabama and traveled about another 7 miles (11 km) before setting up camp for the night. The next morning Crockett and Gibson agreed to split up the party so they could cover more ground. The plan was to have Gibson pass by the home of Dick Brown, a friendly Cherokee, while Crockett would look for Brown's father to see what he knew of the Creek's intentions. After each group gathered as much advanced intelligence from the Browns, the scouting parties would rendezvous that night where the roads came together, about 15 miles (24 km) on the other side of the Browns' property.

When Crockett and his men found the elder Brown, he did not really have any useful information on the whereabouts and plans of the Creek. The only thing to do was follow the plan to meet up with Gibson's party at the designated meeting point. When

Crockett arrived, there was no sign of Gibson or his men. With nightfall approaching, Crockett decided to move the men off the main road and set up camp for the night. The following morning, Crockett had to make his first military decision. Gibson was a no-show, and some of the men feared that the major's party had encountered the Creek and had been killed. Some of them felt they would be no match against an attack and wanted to head back to Beaty's Spring. Crockett reminded them what they had signed on to do, later writing in his autobiography, "I told the men we had set out to hunt a fight, and I wouldn't go back in that way; that we must go ahead, and see what the red men were at."

With no reinforcements to come to their aid, Crockett led his men all the more quietly along the road for about 20 miles (32 km). Around noon, ever so dangerously close to the Creek Nation border, they came upon the home of a white man named Radcliffe. He was married to a Creek woman and had two sons. Because of his wife, Radcliffe had managed to live there in tenuous peace with his Creek neighbors. He was most hospitable to Crockett's men, feeding them and tending to their horses, but nervous throughout their stay. Radcliffe explained that just a short time before Crockett's arrival he had been "visited" by 10 war-painted warriors who would have slaughtered them all if they had come upon them at his house.

Again, some of the men got jittery at the prospect of coming upon the war-hungry Red Stick. Crockett knew he had come out on the scouting mission for a reason and was not going to turn back. So he had all the men mount their horses and forge ahead in search of a camp of friendly Creek about 8 miles (13 km) from the Radcliffe house. They had not gotten very far when they came upon two black men riding Native American ponies, carrying nice rifles. They were slaves that had been forcibly taken by the Native Americans but had managed to escape and were trying to get back to their white owners. Crockett sent one of the slaves back to Ditto's Landing and asked the other to assist him in his search for the friendly Creek camp. It was evening before they finally found the camp of about 40 Creek men, women, and children.

Kentucky Long Rifle

The Kentucky Long Rifle did not come from Kentucky and it was not used just by Kentuckians. German immigrants crafted it in Lancaster, Pennsylvania, sometime in the 1730s. The single-shot, longer, narrowed barrel of the rifle was lethal at a range of 200 yards (183 m), making it ideal for hunting or defense. The Kentucky Long was often used by frontiersmen and scouts who often dressed in buckskin attire—clothes made from the hides of the male deer. Many of these men, like Davy Crockett, who served in militias and volunteer armies, were feared by the enemy because of their expert marksmanship. During the American Revolutionary War, George Washington made it a point of recruiting men who owned this rifle to use as snipers to pick off unsuspecting British soldiers who were too far away to see the enemy. Crockett's Kentucky Long was especially handy when his militia was ferreting out Creek in the swamps of Florida. Running low on food, Crockett used his expert hunting skills to kill enough wild game to keep the men from starving.

Crockett and his men spent the night in the company of these friendly Creek. Crockett even engaged in shooting arrows with a few of the boys before settling into an uneasy sleep, with his rifle in his arms. His unease was quickly validated when a Native American messenger ran into the camp screaming that the Red Stick were on their way. Worse still, he told Crockett that a large party of Red Stick had been traveling across the Coosa River near a place called Ten Islands (present-day Gadsden, Alabama) on their way to engage General Jackson and his men in battle. Knowing that he now had important intelligence from the scouting expedition, Crockett wanted to get back to Beaty's Spring as quickly as possible. With the imminent danger approaching, the Creek gathered up what they could and scattered, while Crockett and his men mounted their horses and began the dangerous 65-mile (105-km) ride back to Ditto's Landing.

On their way back to the camp at Beaty's Spring, Crockett and his men stopped at Radcliffe's house, only to find it empty. As they reached the outskirts of the nearby town, they could see a blazing fire licking the night sky. The warring Red Stick had set the town on fire. Pushing on throughout the night, the men stopped only briefly at Dick Brown's house to feed and water their horses and grab something to eat. The Crockett scouting party reported back to Colonel Coffee's camp at about 10:00 that morning. Though bone tired and sore from riding all night, Crockett dismounted his horse and went to Coffee with his news. To Crockett's utter amazement, Colonel Coffee seemed to take his report with indifference. "He didn't seem to mind my report a bit, and this raised my dander higher than ever; but I knowed I had to be on my best behaviour, and so I kept it all to myself; though I was so mad that I was burning inside like a tar-kiln, and I wonder that the smoke hadn't been pouring out of me at all points," he recalled in *Narrative*.

Crockett's anger returned the next morning when Coffee responded immediately upon Major Gibson's return to camp with the same news, spewing forth with theatrics and histrionics that would have made an acting troupe proud. Coffee ordered the men to erect a temporary fortification wall at least a quarter mile (about 400 m) in length around the camp. Crockett's anger quickly turned to bitterness when Coffee also dispatched a rider to General Jackson with the news of the impending Red Stick attack. In Crockett's mind, Coffee had not taken his news as seriously as he had Gibson's because he was not an officer, just merely a poor volunteer soldier. It never occurred to him that Coffee might not have given his news the same weight because it was based on hearsay. What the experience did instead was plant firmly in Crockett's thinking that the armed service was merely a caste (a social order) system like any other. That feeling became a sore spot for Crockett that remained throughout his life.

FINALLY SEEING BATTLE

General Andrew Jackson and his army arrived in camp the next day. The fortification wall would not be necessary as Jackson was itching to get into battle. Dubbed "Old Hickory" by his men because of his toughness and unwillingness to give in to anything, Jackson believed the best defense was a strong offense. He wanted to intercept the Creek to the south and engage them before they could initiate an attack. Now, early in November, Crockett was about to see his first action. Jackson led his formidable force out of the camp at Beaty's Spring toward the same route Crockett's men had followed on their scouting mission. At the Tennessee River, Jackson split up his forces, sending 800 men including Crockett under the command of Colonel Coffee to present-day Tuscaloosa and on to Black Warrior Town. After stopping to stock up on food and water at the abandoned town, Coffee led his men to meet up with Jackson's forces at almost the same location Crockett and Gibson were to have met up after leaving the Browns. Jackson's men were in need of food, so Crockett volunteered to hunt for game. The skillful hunter and marksman returned with a freshly killed deer, supplying enough meat for the men to fill their hungry bellies.

The next day, the convened armies came upon a less-than-friendly Radcliffe who was home and not so eager to share his stockpile of food. Radcliffe had a terrible secret that was later revealed: He had sent the screaming Native American into Crockett's Creek-friendly camp with a made-up story about the Red Stick being on their way to Ten Islands. Radcliffe had come up with the scheme to get the scouting party away from his house and to return to camp with a false story. The men promised revenge and later returned to force Radcliffe's two sons into army service. Leaving Radcliffe's, the armies forged on to Ten Islands and erected fortifications to set up camp. Several scouts were sent out to acquire reliable information on the Red Stick whereabouts. Some of the scouts returned with news that a large group of Creek were settled in Tallusahatchee, just 8 miles (13 km) away.

Newly promoted Brigadier General Coffee split his army into two groups to line along each side of town, eventually encircling the Creek and trapping them. The battle was won before it began as 900 troops to 180 Creek would have been a slaughter. Most of the Creek simply surrendered. However, a smaller band refused to put down their weapons and went on the attack before barricading themselves into the nearby houses. Crockett and his men went after a group of about 46 Creek holed up in one structure. Before they had time to react, a Creek squaw drew her bow and shot an arrow, killing one of the volunteers. It was the first time Crockett had seen someone killed with a bow and arrow. Rage ensued as Crockett described the scene:

> We now shot them like dogs; and then set the house on fire, and burned it up with the forty-six warriors in it. I recollect seeing a boy who was shot down near the house. His arm and thigh was broken, and he was so near the burning house that the grease was stewing out of him. In this situation he was still trying to crawl along; but not a murmur escaped him, though he was only about twelve years old. So sullen is the Indian, when his dander is up, that he had sooner die than make a noise or ask for quarters.

In all, about 185 Red Stick were killed or taken prisoner. Coffee lost just five men.

Low again on provisions, Crockett and his men returned to the scene of the battle. The sight of the dead and the burned buildings was even more gruesome in the light of day. Provisions were getting scarce and the men were getting weak from lack of food. The men did find a stockpile of potatoes, but there was no rest for the weary as word came that a large group of Red Stick had surrounded Fort Talladega, which was about 30 miles (48 km) from camp. Jackson ordered all the men to their feet, weapons ready, to march out. It was sunrise by the time the troops arrived at the fort. Crockett noted about 1,100 painted Creek outside the fort trying to convince the friendly Creek inside to join them in the fight against Jackson.

Using the same tactic as Coffee had the day before at Tallusahatchee, Jackson ordered his men to encircle the warriors with two lines of soldiers and slowly decrease the space between warrior and soldier until the Red Stick were trapped. When two of the friendly

Creek inside the fort jumped outside onto a horse to warn the troops of the danger of hundreds of Creek hidden in the brush ahead, bedlam erupted. Native Americans and soldiers came together amid a mass of flying bullets and arrows. In man-to-man clashes, tomahawks and swords inflicted deadly wounds. The encircled line of soldiers parted, allowing more than 700 Red Stick to escape through the gap in the line. This tactical error cost Jackson the opportunity to put a quick end to the war. Had they been contained, the Red Stick would have been defeated, and Madison's objective of heading off a growing uprising would have been achieved with little loss of American lives.

Weary from battle, having only limited supplies and food, and being on the hunt for nearly three months, Crockett and many of the other volunteer soldiers wanted to go home. Some of Jackson's men had been with him since his Natchez expedition back in January 1813 and were still in service past the time they had signed on for duty. They wanted to go home, get rested, get new clothes, fresh horses, eat their fill, and return in better shape ready for another campaign of fighting. Jackson was defiant, however, and no one was relieved of duty. Though there were a few anxious moments and rumblings of a possible mutiny, Jackson's intimidating, fiery temperament kept the men in line. A few weeks later, Jackson relented and allowed the men to go home for two weeks before reporting back on December 8.

Polly was glad to see her husband return, and Crockett was happy to be home to spend time with his wife and kids. When Polly found out Crockett would be leaving again in just a few weeks, however, her happiness turned to irritation. Though Crockett was once again torn about leaving, he was an honorable man who kept his word. Despite Polly's objections, Crockett returned to his unit to finish out his official duty until it expired on December 24, 1813. He stayed on a while after his tour was up, joining the command of Major William Russell. Crockett was engaged in a few battles, including the skirmish at Alabama's Emuckfaw Creek, where four volunteers were killed and several others wounded, and Enitachopco Creek, where only the rallying of men by Colonel William

After the defeat of the Creek, Andrew Jackson forced the tribe to sign the Treaty of Fort Jackson, which forced the Creek Nation to give up 23 million acres of their land to the U.S. government. The Creek that fought alongside Jackson's troops during the Battle of Horseshoe Bend objected to the treaty, but Jackson saw no difference between the two groups. Above, William "Chief Red Eagle" Weatherford surrenders to Jackson.

Carroll made a stand long enough for Coffee's men to drive the Creek into a retreat.

Rattled by the fighting at Enitachopco Creek, Crockett decided that he had enough fighting with the Native Americans and got a furlough to go home. In doing so, he missed the decisive battle with the Red Stick at Horseshoe Bend (Tohopeka) on March 27, 1814. Jackson cemented his image in the military as an outstanding commander with the crushing defeat of the Creek, thereby ending their involvement in the war. As for Crockett, he was returning home to renew his work on the farm. Nonetheless, the war with the British continued, and soon Crockett would be back serving in the military. Instead of hunting Red Stick, he would be hunting Redcoats.

HARSH REALITIES
OF WAR AND LIFE

Though glad to be home from the war against the Creek and able to spend time with his wife and children, Crockett had never been cut out to be a farmer. He much preferred to be out in the woods hunting, riding on horseback exploring the wilderness before him, or just sitting under a tree taking in the calm and quiet of nature. Crockett spent time with his sons, sometimes just playing with them when chores on the farm were finished and he had no other pressing responsibilities. He also took the boys into the woods with him to begin to teach them how to track animals and shoot a rifle, all the while telling them in grand fashion about his adventures serving in the 2nd Regiment and fighting Native peoples.

During the winter of 1814, Crockett did as much hunting as he could to store up enough food for the family until the spring thaw. He planted some crops for early harvesting, as he tried to secure enough provisions for Polly and the kids before the war called for his return. Crockett knew he would get back into the fray, because as much as he was weary of the fighting and killing with the Creek, he missed the exhilaration of having a challenge versus the mundane day-to-day on the farm. Being a soldier gave Crockett the chance to be outdoors on horseback, scouting, hunting, tracking—using his frontiersman skills, which he much preferred to his (lack of) farming competency. Soldiers' pay was another incentive, for it was more than he earned harvesting his crops. So, on September 28, 1814, Crockett mounted up his horse again and signed on as a member of the Separate Battalion of Tennessee Mounted Gunmen.

The battalion served from September 1814 to March 1815. Under the command of Major William Russell this group came from various counties of Tennessee including Franklin, Bedford, Blount, Rutherford, Warren, and Wilson, plus Madison, Alabama. Men from fewer Tennessee counties reenlisted than the original group that Crockett was a part of for the Creek campaign. According to the Tennessee State Library article "Regimental Histories of Tennessee Units During the War of 1812," the Separate Battalion of Tennessee Mounted Gunmen unit was assigned to certain areas of the Florida region:

> Along with a battalion commanded by Major Chiles, this unit served in the Pensacola/Mobile region and was a part of Major Uriah Blue's expedition that roamed along the Escambia River in Florida in search of renegade Creeks toward the end of the war. Approximately 500 men served in this battalion, one of whom was David Crockett, a sergeant in Capt. John Conway's company.

From Fayetteville, where the battalion was mustered, the men traveled to Fort Stephens (crossing the Tennessee River at Muscle Shoals); leaving their horses behind, the battalion marched to Pensacola (via Fort Montgomery) where they participated in the battle of November 7, 1814, and then returned to Fort Montgomery. At Fort Montgomery they were put under the command of Major Uriah Blue.

General Andrew Jackson had led his troops brilliantly in bringing an end to the threat of a prolonged war with the Creek. However, a small group of resilient Creek led by Peter McQueen and others still loyal to Tecumseh had fled to the southern panhandle of Pensacola, Florida, to seek refuge with the Spanish.

There the Spanish had allowed several hundred British Redcoats (troops) to come ashore into town and to Fort Barrancas to arm and train the Creek who wanted to continue to fight. The Creek knew the chance for victory and driving the white man out of their lands had been lost, but these dedicated Red Stick were willing to die for the cause and take as many Americans with them as they could. The terrain in and around Pensacola was filled with mangrove swamps (a large, complicated jumble of trees and roots found in coastal wetlands), an ideal landscape for the Creek to attack the unsuspecting enemy. "Old Hickory" Jackson was incensed and wanted the Panhandle mopped clean of any remaining threat from the Native Americans.

SURVIVAL IS BIGGEST BATTLE

Crockett's itch to fight some Redcoats was dashed before he had a chance to engage the enemy. Before his company could get to Pensacola to battle the British, General Jackson had beaten them to the intended targets. In a bloodless encounter, Jackson's men had taken a Spanish-controlled fortification with little resistance from the 500 poorly armed troops inside. Jackson was also thwarted in his desire for a serious battle at Fort Barrancas, as the British and the Spanish still at the fort fled to their ships anchored in Pensacola Bay. When he arrived, fresh for another attack, Jackson could only watch as the ships sailed into the distance. The British had taken care of the fort, too, blowing it up and rendering it useless to the Americans.

Off to fight elsewhere, Jackson and his troops left Pensacola and headed west. Just slightly more than a year later, "Old Hickory" led the Americans into the Battle of New Orleans. It was the defining battle of the War of 1812, and its victory ensured Andrew Jackson a soldier's glory and fame that he would ride into a successful political career. In the meantime, the remaining enemy Creek still needed to be rounded up or killed and that assignment was left to Major Russell and his men.

A contingent of about 1,000 soldiers that included Crockett set out to "mop up" the Pensacola panhandle. The duty carried neither

Although Crockett took part in the battles of the Creek War, including the ruthless battle of Tallusahatchee, he was not an enthusiastic fighter. In fact, later he opposed the Indian Removal Act, gaining the reputation as a friend of the Cherokee. This painting depicts Crockett with two Native Americans.

the heightened anticipation of battle nor the glamour of a major assignment, but Crockett was an experienced woodsman, scout, and hunter, and he certainly had the much-needed skills Major Russell sought. Along with 15 others, including Russell, and some Native American scouts, recently promoted Third Sergeant Crockett gathered up his provisions and moved toward the dark waters and

hidden undergrowth of the mangrove swamps. The terrain was unlike any he had ever seen. The landscape was dotted with salty lakes
and marshy areas, making the ground appear to be submerged.
The mangrove trees rose out of the water, a twisted knot of trunks
choked by shrubs and vines. It was a slow, wet process to maneuver
through these swamps.

After reaching the pine hills beyond the swamps, the men built a
fire to dry off from their submerged journey. Each time the soldiers
moved closer to where there were reports of enemy Creek, their
Native American scouts seemed to have already killed and scalped
them. What soon became more of a concern to the men than the
sporadic enemy encounters was their quickly depleting provisions.
Having left with enough supplies to last 20 days, being gone nearly
twice that long had left the men in dire need of food. Major Russell sent Crockett into the woods and streams in search of food. He
found very little that would significantly change their hunger and
growing weakness. Once, he was fortunate enough to come upon a
large buck, and the fresh kill from his rifle was food that came none
too soon.

Like a child drawn to its protective mother, the men continued to move homeward toward Fort Strother. Close to starvation
and certain death, a true miracle happened. Crockett's group
stumbled upon some East Tennessee troops headed to Mobile,
Alabama. Crockett's brother Joseph was among them. A joyous
reunion was followed by shared provisions for his men and an
evening of shared stories of exaggerated and true adventures.

The following morning, refreshed and stronger, Crockett's men
thanked their fellow Tennesseans and headed home. Crockett took
a few days to rest once he reached Fort Strother. During that time
he reflected on the worth of his latest duty and the toll it had taken
on him. He recognized the real dangers he had subjected himself
to—hostile Native Americans and a real battle for survival in the
unfamiliar and harsh wilds of the Florida Panhandle. Crockett had
his fill of soldiering and fighting. He was ready to return home, this
time for good.

HOMECOMING TURNS TRAGIC

When Crockett reached the boundary of his property and arrived at the cabin he built near Bean's Creek, his weariness soon lifted. The familiar beach tree trunk was still scarred by the initials he had carved into it from when he first settled the family there. Polly and the children waited with anticipation to welcome him home. He fondly recalled the reunion in his book *Narrative:*

> I found them all well and doing well; and though I was only a rough sort of a backwoodsman, they seemed mighty glad to see me, however little the quality folks might suppose it. For I do reckon we love as hard in the backwood country, as any people in the whole of creation.

Not long after he had been home, Crockett received service orders once more, this time to join an expedition going to Alabama to search for more Native Americans. Since Crockett had more than enough of war and wanted to get back to working his farm and spending time with his family, he bought off the remainder of his tour of duty to a wide-eyed young man searching for perhaps the same opportunity for adventure. This action brought to a close the soldiering career of Davy Crockett. He was happy to be home and looked forward to reconnecting with his children and sharing his life with Polly. Unfortunately, Crockett's life changed drastically when Polly became ill and died sometime during 1815. It is not clear what caused her illness, though many afflictions were common on the frontier including malaria, cholera, and typhoid.

Crockett was devastated by Polly's death. Still, he accepted her death as the will of God and immediately turned his attention to the well-being of his children. In his autobiography, he poured out his feelings:

> I met with the hardest trial which ever falls to the lot of man. Death, that cruel leveller of all distinctions—to

whom the prayers and tears of husbands, and of even helpless infancy, are addressed in vain—entered my humble cottage, and tore from my children an affectionate good mother, and from me a tender and loving wife. And as painful as is even yet the remembrance of her sufferings, and the loss sustained by my little children and myself, yet I have no wish to lift up the voice of complaint.

FINDING A NEW WIFE

Crockett knew he could not manage three children on his own, for nothing he had done in his adventurous life outside the home had prepared him to do so. The boys, now eight and six, had probably helped Polly with little chores while Crockett was away; they missed the nurturing only their mother could give. Little Margaret was still a toddler at just three years old and needed more supervision than Crockett could give. Meanwhile, he was still addressing the boys' needs and the farm, and dealing with his own grief. Determined to keep the family together, Crockett convinced his younger brother John and sister-in-law to move in with him to give Crockett and the children time to grieve and to help out around the farm.

Once Crockett got his bearings again, he knew he would need to find another wife and a mother for his children. The motto by which Crockett is linked, which is typed on the title page of *Davy Crockett's Own Story as Written by Himself; the Autobiography of America's Great Folk Hero,* reads: "I leave this rule for others when I'm dead, Be always sure you're right—then go ahead!" This was the philosophy by which Crockett made his decisions. Think things through, know all of your options, and when you are sure of your decision, go forward with it. Although he did not have the greatest record in his courting of women, this time Davy was not looking for love. He was looking more for someone who would benefit from being with him while at the same time he would benefit by being with her—

a partnership without the passion of the butterflies in the stomach and the heart pounding, but one of mutual respect and support.

Elizabeth Patton lived near the Crockett farm. A widow with two preteen children, Patton had lost her husband in the massacre at Fort Mims. Her father, Robert, had served honorably in the American Revolutionary War and later became a successful farmer in North Carolina. Patton had tended well to her small farm, but still was a woman alone on the frontier with children to raise and protect. Surely a man would be a welcomed addition in her life, Crockett thought, and he made up his mind to call on Elizabeth frequently. In time both found the other's company pleasing enough and, in time, came to a mutual agreement to marry. In 1815, they had a small wedding, with a select group of friends and family in attendance at Robert Patton's house.

AN ALMOST FATAL EXCURSION

With the family expanded to seven from their union and feeling the need for more room, Crockett's feet once again became itchy to move on to a new place. He decided it was time to go on a scouting mission to search for "greener pastures" on which to lay claim. He even convinced a few friends to go with him. Setting out with hopeful intentions, Crockett and neighbors he listed in his book as Robinson, Frazier, and Rich could not have imagined how badly things would turn. First, Frazier fell ill from a poisonous snake bite. Assuring them that he would be okay, Frazier told the men to go on without him. After a day's ride, the three men set up camp for the night, but had tied the horses too loosely and the horses wandered away.

In the morning daylight, Crockett left camp on foot to retrieve the horses. His trek took him through swamps and shallow creeks swarming with all kinds of flying, biting insects. He did not realize how far he had traveled in search of the horses and by nightfall was more than 50 miles (80 km) from camp. A kind family took a very weary Crockett in, fed him, and gave him a place to rest for the night. When he awoke in the morning, Crockett felt worse than the day before, his body aching and his legs so weak they could hardly

In 1817, Crockett rode west to explore and found the headwaters of Shoal Creek. He moved his family there, to Lawrenceburg, Tennessee, and built a gristmill, a powdermill, and a distillery. The land where he built his businesses, now known as Davy Crockett State Park, houses a museum (*above*), a campground with bike trails, a restaurant, and recreational activities.

hold him up. Still he was intent on getting back to the others. After thanking the family for the hospitality, Crockett left to backtrack and find Robinson and Rich. The more Crockett walked, the worse he felt. He broke into a cold sweat, his head pounded with each laborious step, and he became unsteady on his feet. Not able to go on, Crockett lay down alongside the road and passed out.

When Crockett awoke, he was disoriented and shaky. A few friendly Creek came upon him and, seeing him ill, walked him to the nearest house. The woman of the house took Crockett in, who by now raged with fever and floated in and out of consciousness. He stayed at the house for a few days, but was not getting any better. Crockett did not know it, but he had contracted malaria, a serious illness caused by a parasite that is transmitted by the bite of a mosquito. A few of Crockett's neighbors, themselves out looking for new land to settle, stopped by the house. They took Crockett with them and rode back to Black Warrior Creek to find Robinson and Rich. By the time Crockett got back to his friends, his condition had turned grave. Robinson and Rich realized Crockett was in no condition to travel, so they took him to a home nearby and left him in the care of the homeowner, Jesse Jones. With home remedies and two weeks of rest, Crockett recovered.

Making his way home by hitching a ride with a wagoner and then by a horse that he purchased from the wagoner, Crockett arrived home to those who thought they were looking at a ghost. Elizabeth had been told her husband had died. When she opened the door to their cabin, seeing Crockett standing there, she was filled with a host of emotions. She was relieved, shocked, and concerned because Crockett looked so bad. In *Life of David Crockett the Original Humorist and Irrepressible Backwoodsman,* George Edward Woodberry wrote how Crockett described his appearance, "I was so pale, and so much reduced, that my face looked like it had been half soled with paper."

While Crockett spent the next several months regaining his strength from the episode of malaria, he was nagged by the continued wanderlust within him to leave Bean's Creek for better land. Learning of the government deal to acquire land of the Chickasaw tribe in south-central Tennessee—which was made possible by Andrew Jackson's treaty with the Chickasaw in September 1816—Crockett decided that was where he wanted to move his family. In the fall of 1817, after the harvest, it was time to leave Bean's Creek and make a fresh start in a place called Shoal Creek.

TRIUMPHS AND SETBACKS

Shoal Creek, in Lawrence County, Tennessee, was about 80 miles (128 km) west of Bean's Creek. The area near the creek was raw and unsettled. Davy and Elizabeth chose a spot to settle near the headwaters of Shoal Creek because of its untouched beauty and closeness to the clean, gently running stream. Davy built a cabin for his growing family—in addition to the five children combined from their first marriages, Elizabeth and Davy had four more children over a period of five years, Robert Patton (1816), Elizabeth Jane (1818), Rebeckah Elvira (1819), and Matilda (1821).

The Shoal Creek area had much promise. With fertile, untouched land, a running stream, and beds of iron ore, there were many opportunities to make money off the natural resources the area provided. Eventually, Crockett would run a gristmill and operate a distillery for making liquor, an iron-ore mine, and a gunpowder factory. With so much opportunity to really be successful for the first time in his life, Crockett felt comfortable that moving to Shoal Creek had been a good decision.

When the Crocketts settled in the county, there were no laws in place. As more and more people populated the area, it became

Although Crockett did not have a legal education, the people of Lawrenceburg were happy with the job Crockett was doing as justice of the peace and magistrate. Most disputes were handled using common sense and fairness. He soon embarked on a political career.

necessary to establish a formal type of government. As with any place, some of the new residents were unsavory characters that stirred up problems and needed to be dealt with. The county was officially established in 1817 by an act of the Tennessee General Assembly. Because the area needed someone to enforce lawfulness, on November 25, 1817, Crockett was elected the first justice of the peace. In his job he would oversee the settling of disputes that ranged from quarrels between couples to unpaid debts. More serious offenses, like stealing a cow from a herd, required more than just a fine. "If anyone was charged with marking his neighbour's hogs, or with stealing anything, which happened pretty often in those days,—I would have him taken, and if there was tolerable grounds for the charge, I would have him well whip'd and cleared," Crockett recalled in *Narrative*.

A NEW CAREER

Folks were very pleased with the job Crockett was doing as magistrate. Even though he was not a trained lawyer, he used his common sense and honesty in all decisions for administering fines and punishments. The people of Lawrence County felt he was a man of integrity and fairness. He had a good-natured sense of humor and could tell stories so well that he had people always coming back to listen to more.

Crockett was soon asked to run for the position of major of the local militia along with a man named Captain Matthews, who would run for lieutenant colonel. Initially, Crockett hesitated to get involved again in the military, but Matthews convinced him to go for it. When Crockett discovered some scheming on Matthews's part to get his son elected instead, Crockett decided to challenge Captain Matthews for the position of lieutenant colonel. He campaigned in a straight-from-the-hip style, speaking to crowds as one of them, and people responded to him. When the votes were tallied, Crockett had soundly defeated Matthews. On November 27, 1818, Davy Crockett became lieutenant colonel of the 57th Regiment of

Militia. It was a glorious moment for him, and the beginning of a budding political career.

Continuing to build on his career in public service, Crockett also served as one of Lawrence County's commissioners, working on a variety of projects. Some of the tasks included identifying boundaries in land claims, compiling a list of existing properties subject to taxation, and gathering statistics on residents for future census use. Over the next two years, Crockett also kept busy with his own growing business ventures. He had come in contact with many of the folks living in the county and had established a good reputation that enabled him to take the next step in the political arena.

In late 1820, Crockett was approached to run for a seat in the Tennessee state legislature. He knew this would mean far more campaigning than he had ever done and raising money to finance his candidacy. It also meant he would be away from his family for stretches of time, and he would have to leave the oversight of the businesses to Elizabeth. He talked it over with Elizabeth and the kids, laying out the pros and cons of such a decision. Ultimately, and with the family's blessing, Crockett decided to run. On January 1, 1821, he resigned as commissioner of Lawrence County and began to plan his campaign.

Crockett ran his campaign for the legislature in the same style as he had when he ran for lieutenant colonel. He never tried to pretend to be something he was not. He was honest with the voters when he told them he knew very little about government and policy, but that he would always be open and tell the truth about a circumstance whether it was difficult or not. He explained that there would be times when a vote on an issue might be unpopular with some of his constituents, but he would always thoroughly study an item before deciding how he would vote.

The first real challenge for Crockett was when he had to speak in front of a large crowd at a frolic (reaping). Feeling uncomfortable, Crockett stammered nervously. How to start? What to say? He struggled for a few moments and then suddenly just decided to do what he did best, as he recounted in *Narrative*:

Crockett was a great storyteller, which made him popular with his neighbors. He was convinced to run for the state legislature (*depicted making a speech, above*) and handily won the election in August 1821.

At last I told them I was like a fellow I had heard of not long before. He was beating on the head of an empty barrel near the roadside, when a traveler, who was passing along, asked him what he was doing that for? The fellow replied, that there was some cider in that barrel a few days before, and he was trying to see if there was any then, but if there was he couldn't get at it. I told them that there had been a little bit of a speech in me a while ago, but I believed I couldn't get it out.

Crockett used this approach in talking to voters throughout the rest of the campaign. Telling funny stories about himself and suggesting that folks have a drink of whiskey seemed to win over the crowds. Crockett read the voters correctly. When all the ballots were counted up on a summer night in August 1821, he was declared the winner. He had just been elected a representative to the 14th Tennessee General Assembly. He was packing his bags and heading for a new adventure, this time to Murfreesboro, the state's capital.

A Voice for the Poor

When Crockett took his seat in the legislature on September 17, 1821, he was representing the folks of two counties—Hickman and Lawrence. He was appointed to the Committee of Propositions and Grievances. The committee suited him as it took up many of the same issues—debt collection, land ownership disputes, and divorces—that he had dealt with as a justice of the peace.

Although his first term was rather unexciting, he did have the opportunity to bring attention to some of the issues he felt strongly about, including reforms concerning land rights and becoming the voice of the poor, the homeless, and the oppressed.

One proposed law Crockett vocally opposed involved land that the Congress was making available in western Tennessee. The area was part of Crockett's district and where many of his constituents lived. Congress proposed that the land go to Revolutionary War veterans. If the law passed, it meant that those who had already settled there and developed the land, like Crockett himself, might have to vacate. In any voting issue, Crockett always cast his where it would help his constituents, mostly poor farmers and settlers, and against any proposed legislation that would negatively affect them.

Soon Crockett had his own woes to deal with. He got terrible news from home that heavy rains and flash flooding had washed away much of his business properties. The gunpowder factory and the gristmill were gone. Crockett had always thought if any danger was to come to the complex it would have been from an explosion in the gunpowder factory. Instead he suffered the same disaster his father had many years before. He had used Elizabeth's money to build the mill and had received a loan on the rest of the complex. What he thought would provide some income for the family was now gone. Crockett was grateful and amazed at how well Elizabeth handled the loss. Before he even had a chance to mull over his options, his honest and straight-forward wife told him to just face the problem head-on and not skip out on his financial obligations. Crockett shared his wife's advice and his own thoughts about the situation in *Narrative:*

> "Just pay up, as long as you have a bit's worth in the world; and then everybody will be satisfied, and we will scuffle for more." This was just such talk as I wanted to hear, for a man's wife can hold him devlish uneasy, if she begins to scold, and fret, and perplex him, at a time when he has a full load for a rail-road car on his mind already.
>
> And so, you see, I determined not to break full handed, but thought it better to keep a good con-science with an empty purse, than to get a bad opinion of myself, with a full one. I therefore gave up all I had, and took a bran-fire new start.

MOVING ON

Forced to sell off what was salvageable, Crockett paid his creditors in full. When he returned to Murfreesboro, he had already decided that he needed to move the family again. The ever-steady and strong Elizabeth was left to pack their belongings for the time they would leave Shoal Creek and move even farther south and west within Tennessee. On November 17, 1821, Crockett officially completed his first session as a Tennessee legislator. He had made a few "professional" friends, including William Carroll, a close political and personal friend of Andrew Jackson.

Once back at Shoal Creek, Crockett packed up some provisions and enlisted the assistance of his eldest son, John Wesley, and

Crockett's life on the frontier was legendary, even in his day. Dramatic accounts of his bravery and skill in the wilderness tell of events that seem unbelievable, including a story about his killing 105 bears in less than one year. In this painting, Crockett faces down two grizzly bears.

a neighbor, Abraham Henry, to make the journey with him. Their destination was land near the Obion River, an area near present-day Rutherford, Tennessee, and a good 150 miles (240 km) from Shoal Creek.

During his time there, Crockett did what he loved best—hunt. The area was so sparsely settled that the wild animal population seemed larger than the human one. Of course the hunting was also a necessity if the Crockett family was going to eat and have warm clothing. Crockett's hunting was so successful that he had abundant food from the bear, deer, and wolves he killed. He sold wolf hides when he needed the income.

With the help of his son and a hired hand who went by the name Flavius Harris, Crockett constructed a cabin and cleared the wild field around it so that it could be planted. He also stored a huge amount of dried bear meat and venison from his hunts before heading back to Shoal Creek to Elizabeth and the other children. After an abbreviated session of the legislature called by newly elected governor William Carroll adjourned (April 22 to August 24, 1822), Crockett had completed his elected term. Returning home, he and Elizabeth gathered up their belongings and the kids to begin the long journey to their new home at Rutherford's Fork. It took them more than a month to travel the 150 miles (240 km).

Once settled again in new surroundings, Crockett spent his legislative recess hunting and preparing for the winter months. During one hunt, Crockett bagged the bear that stories have been told about over and over. It was the largest bear he had ever seen and it took several shots to kill. Crockett recounted in his autobiography that the bear must have weighed 600 pounds (272 kilograms).

Wild animals were so plentiful that Crockett had little trouble accumulating several pelts to sell at the trading post in Jackson, Tennessee. During one such trip, Crockett and his son John Wesley stopped in the local saloon to have a drink with some old soldier buddies from his Creek War days. There were a few local officials in the saloon too who were talking about their candidacies for the legislature. One man, Dr. William Butler, was well connected to Andrew Jackson, having married Jackson's niece. The other two were also known politicians. The men suggested that Crockett ought to run, too. He told them he really did not want to be involved in government anymore.

A few weeks after the visit at the saloon, a neighbor of Crockett's came by with the county paper to show him that he was listed as a candidate. Crockett was furious and thought the men were playing games with him. But if they wanted a game, he was willing to play *and* win. It meant leaving the farm and homestead again to spend time on the campaign trail. His greatest challenge was coming from Andrew Jackson's friend Dr. Butler. Forming what he thought would be his best strategy, Crockett followed Butler to every campaign stop he made and gave his speeches after Butler had spoken.

Crockett already had a reputation and a history with his constituents. The people knew him and liked what he had to say. Even with Jackson's backing, Butler lost to Crockett by 247 votes. The backwoodsman was going to return to Murfreesboro, but was now at odds with one of the party's and the country's most powerful and influential men—Andrew Jackson. Though Crockett had admired the general for his military talent, he had soured on Jackson once he had gotten involved in politics. His dislike for Jackson only deepened when, in 1823, Old Hickory decided to run against U.S. senator John Williams, who was up for reelection and a shoo-in against opposing candidate Pleasant M. Miller. Though Jackson was not really interested in the Senate seat—he was being primed for a presidential run—he thought he could defeat Miller and gain the seat for his party. Crockett voted for Williams because he thought he had done a good job during his term, but made clear his support for Jackson's presidential aspirations.

Jackson won the election by 10 votes, and Crockett had bucked the party line. Not really having any intention of taking the Senate seat, Jackson declined to assume the position. Instead, he had gotten Williams out and would not have to deal with him in any political capacity going forward. Though Crockett clearly established his independence by his vote, he would not gain the support of the Jacksonian Democrats in any future election bids. It would not be long before Crockett would feel the impact of not having Jackson's support.

WINS AND LOSSES

Crockett spent his next term in the Tennessee state legislature continuing to work for the poor folks in his district. For example, he supported a bill to reduce state property taxes and opposed a bill that would allow the use of prisoners to perform manual labor on state-related projects like road repairs. He never softened his stance against any bill that even had the suggestion it might jeopardize the rights of his constituents on lands that were constantly being eyed for sale or development. In one such instance, North Carolina University presented a large number of land warrants belonging to veterans who were now deceased. By bringing these warrants forth, the university administrators wanted to get permission to sell land in the western part of Tennessee to the state as a means of raising money for the school.

The underlying issue of recognizing the warrants from whoever brought them forward remained the same: forcing a large number of squatters to vacate the land, although they were already working it and living in homes they had built. Crockett was among those who could very well be affected by such an approval. The question of whether to grant the university's request split the legislature. Some of Andrew Jackson's supporters, such as Felix Grundy, whom Crockett had already alienated with his vote for Williams over Jackson, supported granting the university the warrants. Others, like James Polk, a firm supporter of Jackson,

During his first term in Congress, Crockett was dedicated to the defense of his poor constituents against land speculators. He was determined to pass a bill granting land to people living as squatters (like this family shown) in western Tennessee.

opposed the idea. Initially, Crockett also opposed it but was concerned that North Carolina residents would just come into Tennessee and purchase the unoccupied land with cash. Either way, the poor farmers who were already there would be forced out, and Crockett did not want to see that happen. He favored allowing those already living on their individual parcel the opportunity to purchase the land on credit. Whatever the outcome of the debate, Crockett clearly demonstrated his commitment to represent the poor and less-fortunate folks in western Tennessee.

DEFEAT AND DISASTER

Even without the backing of the more powerful members of his party, Crockett was very popular with his constituents. In 1824, having successfully regained his seat in the Tennessee legislature, Crockett set his sights on a race against the incumbent congressman, Colonel Adam Alexander. The victor would head to Washington, D.C., to represent the good people of the western district of Tennessee. This was Crockett's first entry into a large campaign and election outside of his area, and he was ill prepared for it, both financially and politically. Though he was well liked in his own local districts, the congressional district covered 18 counties, 11 of which were Alexander country.

To have a chance of winning the election, Crockett had to travel extensively and introduce himself to hundreds of folks who had little knowledge about the woodsman. Alexander had the money to finance a large reelection campaign and the powerful support from members of the party including Felix Grundy, Andrew Jackson, and John Overton, a judge at the Superior Court of Tennessee. One thing Crockett knew from his very first experience with running for public office was his dislike of the politics of political life. Men often forged alliances with each other for leverage or power, or even favors later on. Crockett had chosen not to be a part of the inner circle and lose his independence in voting matters. Unfortunately, in making that choice, Crockett alienated men who could have helped move his political career along.

Political campaigns often turn ugly, with candidates looking for anything to give them an edge over their opponents. Exaggerating negatives or even lying about a candidate's positions on issues was a seedier side of the process. Judge Overton was particularly brutal in his attacks on Crockett, distorting his record in a three-month onslaught. Crockett had neither the finances nor the staff to combat the negative campaign waged by Alexander and his supporters. Crockett lost to Alexander in August 1825 by 267 votes, an election much closer than most key politicians had predicted. Crockett headed home to Elizabeth and the children, out of a job, and for now, out of politics.

MORE CLOSE CALLS

Crockett had always been a good provider for his family. His keen hunting and sharp shooting skills made it possible for him to kill wild game to put food on the table. He was a capable builder, constructing cabins for shelter and fencing to enclose his land to keep what few farm animals he had from wandering away. Still, Crockett had never been successful in farming or in business ventures. He was always looking for the investment or project that was going to make him his fortune. He had also cheated death a few times, such as when he contracted malaria. His latest venture was supposed to earn a good return on his money. Instead, it brought him to yet another life-or-death moment.

The latest business pursuit took Crockett 25 miles (40 km) from home to Obion Lake in Tennessee. Once there he hired men to construct two large flatboats for carrying cargo and a crew down the Obion to the Mississippi River to navigate onward to New Orleans. He intended to sell cut staves—pieces of wood made out of oak planks split by hand and heated to curve slightly—for barrel making. He figured he could earn a good profit with each shipment. Though experienced as a woodsman and hunter, Crockett had no skills on the water. Even that did not deter him or dampen his enthusiasm.

While the boats were being built, Crockett went on a lengthy hunting trip. During this excursion, he had bagged the largest bear he had ever seen, killing it with just his knife. Yet again, while out on the hunt, Crockett found himself in grave danger of dying. This time, alone and soaking wet from a river he had crossed while tracking the bear, Crockett began shivering in the cold. As his body temperature dropped dangerously, he tried to light a fire, but the wood and leaves were green and damp. Crockett was afraid hypothermia was setting in and that soon he would slip into unconsciousness and die. To keep warm, he came up with an interesting exercise, which he described in *Narrative:*

> So I got up, and hollered a while, and then I would just jump up and down with all my might, and throw myself into all sorts of motions. But all this wouldn't do; for my blood was now getting cold, and the chills coming all over me. I was so tired, too, that I could hardly walk; but I thought I would do the best I could to save my life, and then, if I died, nobody would be to blame. So I went to a tree about two feet [0.6 m] through, and not a limb on it for thirty feet [nine m], and I would climb up it to the limbs, and then lock my arms together around it, and slide down to the bottom again. This would make the in-sides of my legs and arms feel mighty warm and good. I continued this till daylight in the morning, and how often I clomb [climb] up my tree and slid down I don't know, but I reckon at least a hundred times.

The constant activity throughout the night kept Crockett warm enough to keep him from freezing.

Having completed another satisfying hunting adventure, Crockett headed home to check on the progress of his barrel-stave business venture. It was mid-January 1826, and the men working on the boats had not only finished constructing them, they had also loaded about 30,000 staves aboard the vessels. The flatboats were rather simple in their design. Unlike other boats that are curved, these were rectangular with a central cabin for sleeping and resting during a long voyage or for shelter in inclement weather. Because of their size and shape, the flatboats were not easily navigable, but the men did their best to find a spot in which to plunge an oar in the water and row them along.

Almost Drowned

The trip along the Obion River started out smoothly and uneventfully until the river converged with the much larger Mississippi about halfway down Tennessee's western border. The "Mighty Mississippi," the second largest river in America, flows 2,320 miles (3,730 km) from its source in Minnesota to its mouth in the Gulf of Mexico. Its waters are much faster than the smaller, slow-flowing Obion. Once the crews maneuvered the boats onto the Mississippi, they quickly lost navigational control. Crockett wrote that upon seeing the river, he was sure he was the most scared of everyone on-board. In a desperate attempt to gain control of the boats as they zigzagged and whirled wildly in the churning water, Crockett tried to tie them together. Instead of steadying the boats, they skimmed sideways and would not react in any way to attempts to navigate or run them aground.

By nightfall, the river slowed, but instead of letting the boats float along through the night, Crockett tried to land them on shore along the bank of the river. Physically exhausted and unsuccessful in every attempt, Crockett finally gave up. Thinking the boats would just continue to float along, he went to the cabin below to rest. Not long after he settled down, he heard shouts and heavy footsteps above. The lead boat had slammed into a tree that pierced into the wooden hull. The dark waters instantly started to suck the boat down. Crockett's boat was next. As the water surged into the boat, he tried to scamper to the hatchway to get on deck, but the boat flipped on its side, leaving Crockett trapped. He quickly remembered a smaller hole that was now overhead and frantically began banging on the wood, trying to make the hole bigger to get out. The men above heard Crockett screaming and tugged and pulled on him until he was finally freed.

A CONGRESSMAN'S TRIALS

Moments after being saved from drowning, Crockett watched the boat sink and disappear. The next morning, the men were rescued by a passing boat and taken into Memphis, where news of their ordeal had preceded them. Among the awaiting crowd that had gathered at the dock was Marcus B. Winchester, a successful businessman who owned department stores. He took Crockett and his crew to his

Although Crockett continued to charm others with his dramatic tales of frontier life, he also remained honest and upstanding. Besides serving as an advocate for poor settlers, Crockett opposed President Jackson's Indian Removal Act and gave a stirring speech critical of his Congressional colleagues that resulted in the termination of a popular proposal. This image depicts Crockett telling tales to Congress.

store and outfitted them with new clothes and then took them to his home where he shared his food with the weary travelers.

Winchester and Crockett got along famously. All the men went into town to party, giving Crockett a willing audience to hear his tales. So impressed by how Crockett charmed people with his charismatic personality, Winchester urged him to run again for Congress and even gave him some money to finance a campaign. Encouraged by Winchester's support and competitive by nature, Crockett welcomed another opportunity to run against Colonel Alexander. Andrew Jackson was making his own run—for the U.S. presidency—and this time Crockett wholeheartedly supported his candidacy.

Andrew Jackson: America's First Working-Class President

The man who became the seventh president of the United States could hardly have had a more different upbringing than the presidents who preceded him. Andrew Jackson was born in a backwoods settlement along the border between North and South Carolina to impoverished Irish immigrants. He excelled less in school subjects than in horseback riding, wrestling, and racing, but the fiery youngster with a quick temper would ultimately earn renown for being a bold general and a determined and controversial leader who passionately believed in the common man.

Left fatherless as a young child, Andrew was an impatient, active, and athletic who disliked school, although he learned to read very well. When the Revolutionary War reached the Carolinas, 13-year-old Andrew joined the militia. He was captured during a British raid in 1781 and endured a 40-mile (64-km) forced march to Camden, South Carolina, nearly starved and sick with smallpox. Though Andrew recovered, his mother, Elizabeth, died shortly after contracting cholera from soldiers she was nursing.

After the war, the newly orphaned teen moved to Salisbury, North Carolina, where he studied law by day and developed a reputation as a troublemaker by night. In 1787, the 20-year-old leaped at the chance to become a public prosecutor in Nashville, Tennessee. The frontier town suited Andrew, and after earning a law license, he was in great demand. He purchased slaves and bought property near Nashville on which he would later build a mansion, which he called the Hermitage.

Eventually, Jackson married and became the first man from Tennessee elected to the House of Representatives. He later served as a U.S. senator, but then resigned his seat and returned to Tennessee. There he was commissioned as major general of the Tennessee militia.

During the War of 1812, Jackson led his troops on an attack against the Red Stick Creek who had killed about 250 American civilians,

(continues)

(continued)

Mississippi militia, and other Creek who had taken refuge at Fort Mims in present-day Alabama. Jackson's Tennessee militia and Native American allies soundly defeated the main Creek force at the Battle of Horseshoe Bend in 1814. Ordered to negotiate a peace treaty with the Creek, Jackson demanded 22 million acres (8.9 million ha) of their land for the U.S. government. He became a national hero.

Jackson later resigned his army commission and was appointed governor of the new Florida Territory. Jackson had higher aspirations, however. Though his first attempt to be elected president of the United States in 1822 failed, he was victorious in 1828. Scandals with his cabinet appointments caused so many problems that it was the first, and last, time in history where an entire cabinet resigned or was fired, forcing an entirely new cabinet to be assembled.

During his two terms in office, Jackson clashed with members of Congress and the Whigs (the opposition party). Among his more controversial proposals were the abolishment of the Electoral College and the uprooting of more than 45,000 Native Americans to lands west of the Mississippi. At the end of his second term in 1837, Jackson retired to his mansion in Tennessee, where he died on June 8, 1845.

Crockett worked hard on his congressional campaign and when the votes were counted, Crockett had defeated Alexander by more than 2,000 votes. Crockett's election in 1827 signaled the appeal of a candidate who was more akin to his constituents than the elitist politicians who had come before him. He had more in common with the everyday folks in the districts he represented, and therefore could relate to their needs and wants because he was one of them. U.S. congressman David Crockett was going to Washington with optimism and energy, but he would soon discover that national politics was very different than the way things worked on the local level. Things in Washington moved very slowly, and it was difficult to get any real work done. He later complained to his friends, revealing an impatient aspect of his personality.

Congressman Crockett's biggest concern in his new job was protecting the interests of his constituents in western Tennessee. He found it difficult to fit in with the more refined politicians in Washington, who did not understand the life of the squatters and other poor residents living in his congressional district. When discussion within a committee chaired by James Polk began, the debate centered on whether to grant the North Carolina University land warrants request or reject it. Polk, who supported to geographic expansion of the country, argued that of the more than 444,000 acres (280,000 ha) provided in the lands once considered part of western North Carolina that were now part of Tennessee, only 22,000 acres (8,900 ha) would remain after honoring the warrants. Crockett disagreed and went further in his impassioned assertion, as quoted in Folmsbee and Catron's *David Crockett: Congressman*:

> The low ground or bottoms, contiguous to the streams in this western division, are frequently from one to two miles in width; but an important reason why they neither are, nor can be, valuable, is . . . that they are usually inundated.

Crockett thought that the rich infrequently needed legislative protection, and that perhaps as responsible lawmakers, legislators should occasionally pass bills to assist the poor. As *American Legend* author Buddy Levy wrote:

> His appeal was that the bill would finally allow these poor farmers to own their own property, the squatters being a class of people that Crockett felt should be compensated for their courage. Crockett considered squatters "the pioneering advance guard of the American nation . . . that in return for their services they were entitled to the plot of land which they had improved, and on which they had made their homes."

Much to Crockett's dismay, the bill was set aside for renewed consideration during the second session the following December. Time at home was unpleasant during the recess as Elizabeth had tired of her husband's long absences and stories of heavy drinking and late-night outings in Washington, D.C. Crockett also continued to struggle with health issues, which some historians speculate were attributable to his bout with malaria. He fared no better upon his return to the nation's capital. More determined to get his bill passed, Crockett added amendments that even his congressional supporters could not go along with. Many more of his fellow Democrats turned against Crockett when rumors began spreading that he was aligning himself more with Republican representatives than with those of his own party. From Crockett's perspective, the only positive thing to come of this latest encounter with national politics was the election of Andrew Jackson as the country's seventh president.

UNDONE BY THE POLITICS OF POLITICS

Crockett won reelection over Colonel Alexander again, winning his congressional seat in August 1829 by more than 3,000 votes. Returning to Washington, D.C., Crockett wasted no time in trying to revive his bill to assist the poor with land warrants, but he met an even stronger wave of opposition. He was really an outsider now, cast out by his own party. Known to hold his own grudges, Crockett began to oppose other legislation put forth, just to be uncooperative. He was not the only one playing politics, and Crockett did not have the stomach for the gamesmanship and self-interest maneuverings. There were several controversies besides the land warrants bill, including Jackson's desire to remove Native Americans from open lands and relocate them. His Indian Removal Act stirred a lot of controversy, passing by a vote of 102–97.

Crockett voted against the bill, the only Tennessee congressman to do so. His no vote was a vote against Jackson and effectively killed any future he might have had in politics. Jackson publically urged Crockett's own constituents not to return him to Congress. Backing a candidate named William Fitzgerald, Jackson and his supporters managed to derail Crockett's reelection. Fitzgerald beat him by 586 votes. The election was not the only thing Crockett had lost. When he returned home, he found the homestead empty of his wife and children. Fed up with his long absences and constant debts, Elizabeth had taken the children to live with the rest of the Patton family in Gibson County, Tennessee. With no friends, family, or political allies, Crockett was on his own and alone again, for the first time since childhood.

THE END OF A POLITICAL CAREER

In 1831, after losing his bid for a third term in Congress, Crockett had time again to work on his farm and try to make some money selling whatever crops he could harvest. His pride was still bruised from Elizabeth's abandonment and the shenanigans of the election against William Fitzgerald. Crockett may not have been the best husband or a successful businessman, but he did have principles and a conscience. He was never a follower, nor did he ever offer just blind allegiance to anyone. The fact that he had clashed with President Andrew Jackson and would not tow the party line was evidence enough of his character.

Even though it had cost him dearly, Crockett never regretted standing for what he believed was right. In *Narrative*, he wrote:

> I was re-elected to Congress, in 1829 . . . and soon after
> . . . I saw, or thought I did, that it was expected of me that
> I was to bow to the name of Andrew Jackson, and fol-
> low him in all his motions, and mindings, and turnings,
> even at the expense of my conscience and judgment.
> Such a thing was new to me, and a total stranger to my
> principles. I know'd well enough, though, that if I didn't

When Andrew Jackson became president of the United States in 1829, he sought to be a direct representative of the common man. Crockett had been supportive of Jackson; however, he did not support many of Jackson's measures and was not able to vote for anything he did not feel was right. Jackson began to be portrayed negatively, as seen by this cartoon depicting Jackson as "King Andrew the First" in 1832.

"hurra" for his name, the hue and cry was to be raised against me, and I was to be sacrificed, if possible. His famous, or rather I should say his infamous Indian bill was brought forward, and I opposed it from the purest motives in the world . . . I believed it was a wicked, unjust measure, and that I should go against it, let the cost to myself be what it might; that I was willing to go with General Jackson in everything that I believed was honest and right; but, further than this, I wouldn't go for him, or any other man in the whole creation; that I would sooner be honestly and politically dead, than hypocritically immortalized.

Because he felt he was right in his stand against some of Jackson's policies, Crockett had no regrets about losing the election other than the dirty tactics the Jackson loyalists had used in the campaign. Back home he found himself unpopular with folks believing he was not looking out for their interests after all—that he was a boozer and a partier and gave little heed to what the majority in Congress was legislating. The tales were not true, but Crockett had few resources and even fewer friends to help defend his reputation. He decided to work on the farm and catch up on all the hunting he had missed while in Washington. He also realized there would be another election in two years, and he was determined to be on the winning side of that one.

RECOGNIZED NATIONALLY

Even though Crockett had come off a tough campaign, he had gained recognition nationally for his outdoor pioneering spirit in the new frontier. Stories of his encounters with bears, his sharpshooting skills, battles with Native Americans, and close calls with death out in the wilds were shared beyond the borders of Tennessee. In New York, playwright James Kirke Paulding had written a story based on a character named Nimrod Wildfire. The play was an offshoot of an earlier piece by William Moncrieff called *Monsieur Mallet* (*My Daughter's Letter*). As quoted in Levy's *American Legend: The Real Life Adventures of David Crockett*, Paulding's character Jeremiah Kentuck was "a bragging, self-confident, versatile and vigorous frontiersman . . . Congressman, attorney-at-law, dealer in-log wood, orator, and half-horse, half-alligator, with a touch of steamboat, and a small taste of the snapping turtle." The similarities to Crockett were impossible to miss, and the actor who played the role of Kentuck wanted a story that was focused on that character. Paulding obliged and wrote *The Lion of the West* for actor James Hackett.

The play was really a parody of Colonel David Crockett, with Hackett running around the stage wildly in his buckskin clothes and fur cap performing some of the more outlandish moments of Crockett's behavior and speeches in Washington. Although it was really a play making fun of the unpolished politician from western Tennessee, the audiences loved the show. Paulding denied that Nimrod Wildfire was drawn from Crockett's life, but audiences forever made the connection of the character to the real-life frontiersman. Crockett was down on his luck but not out. He was going to try to win back his congressional seat.

During the 1833 campaign, running against incumbent William Fitzgerald, a biography was published on Crockett titled *Life and Adventures of Colonel David Crockett of West Tennessee*. The book was a huge success, and his growing prominence helped Crockett move ahead in the polls. On Election Day, August 1833, Crockett narrowly defeated Fitzgerald and headed back to Washington. He got to work again right away on a land bill, making a motion on the House floor to create a committee to determine the best way to deal with the land in western Tennessee. He also decided to write his autobiography. Not the best speller or writer, Crockett requested assistance with the book from his friend Kentucky congressman Thomas Chilton. He titled his compilation of humorous stories, exploits on the frontier, and political career, *A Narrative of the Life of David Crockett of the State of Tennessee*.

Andrew Jackson had been reelected to a second term as president in 1832. He battled with health issues off and on throughout his presidency and chose to retire when his term was up in 1837. The Jacksonian Democrats wanted Vice President Martin Van Buren as their presidential candidate. In 1833, an opposition party formed after being displeased by Jackson's authoritarian rule. The party was known as the Whigs (a British term for royal tyranny) and had several recognized members including Henry Clay, Daniel Webster, William Henry Harrison, and Zachary Taylor. Wanting to put forth a candidate known for his opposition to Andrew Jackson and his policies, the Whigs took a serious look at Congressman Crockett. Crockett had already planned a "book tour" of the Northeast to begin on April 25, 1834. He would make personal appearances in cities including Baltimore, Philadelphia, New York, and Boston. The book tour would serve to test the national support for Crockett to determine if he would be a viable candidate for the party.

The four-city tour may have afforded Crockett a lot of book sales, but it was used against him when it came time for his congressional reelection. Opponents pointed to his three-week absence from the House and his legislative duties, opting for self-promotion on the taxpayer's time and money. Jackson wanted Crockett's land bill to be buried. Holding little back, his forces selected a formidable opponent to run against Crockett. He was a Tennessee lawyer named Adam Huntsman, a veteran of the War of 1812. He was physically disabled, with a wooden leg, but was a great campaigner and speaker. Old political tactics were dusted off, and Huntsman went after Crockett on his rumored heavy drinking and sometimes odd behavior. It was difficult for Crockett to constantly be on the defensive, limiting his speech time for talk about the issues Tennesseans cared most about. He lost to Huntsman by several hundred votes, and with the defeat, saw the end of his political career. Even the Whig Party, which had been so enthusiastic about a Crockett presidential candidacy, seemed suddenly lukewarm to an unelectable Crockett.

OFF TO TEXAS

Declaring that he was "done with politics for the present," Crockett wrote in *Narrative*:

> As my country no longer requires my services, I have made up my mind to go to Texas. My life has been one of danger, toil, and privation, but these difficulties I had to encounter at a time when I considered it nothing more than right good sport to surmount them; but now I start anew upon my own hook, and God only grant that it may be strong enough to support the weight that may be hung upon it. I have a new row to hoe, long and a rough one, but come what will I'll go ahead.

Tennessee had become too crowded for the hunter and frontiersman, and Crockett had heard about the vast openness of the territory of Texas. He also had heard about the rising tensions between the American settlers there and the Mexican government. He was more eager to make a new start in a less populated area than he was to fight someone else's war. The frontiersman in him had always been his most comfortable persona, and he looked ahead to an opportunity to make a fresh start away from politics and failed ventures. Texas was farther away than Crockett had ever ventured, and he looked forward to what he would find in this new territory.

Texas had been part of the larger state of Mexico known as Coahuila and Texas, but now was hankering to be independent from Mexico. Leading the government and the military of Mexico was the cruel and unpredictable ruler General Antonio López de Santa Anna. At the time of Crockett's departure, he knew little about the dictatorship that Santa Anna had imposed on the Mexican people or the general's intention to squash any attempts by others to break Texas free of Mexican control.

Crockett set out for Texas on November 1, 1835, with two of his neighbors, Lindsay Tinkle and Abner Burgin, and his nephew

General Antonio López de Santa Anna sent a letter to President Jackson stating that any Americans that fought the Mexican government would be treated as pirates and that there would be no prisoners of war. On February 23, 1836, 1,500 Mexican troops raised a blood-red flag that signaled no quarter, meaning they would show no mercy.

William Patton. When he left home, he was thinking about the vast open and available land awaiting settlement by men like himself who were looking for a good place to tend a farm and make money off the earth. If he liked what he found in Texas, Crockett planned to bring the family out there. The journey to Texas was going to be as eye-opening as, and more physically demanding than, all of Crockett's previous expeditions to unseen territories he scouted as a hunter and soldier. He was now almost 50 years old, and the route to Texas took Crockett and his traveling companions southwest on horseback and by steamboat. They stopped in Memphis, Tennessee, where in a bar of the Union Hotel during a farewell drinking get-together, Crockett is reported to have made his famous comment, "I told the voters that if they would elect me I would serve them to the best of my ability; but if they did not, they might go to hell, and I would go to Texas. I am on my way now."

The next day the group went to board the Catfish Bay ferry, which would take them across the Mississippi River to Arkansas. Once in the neighboring state, the four men remounted their horses and rode the roughly 130 miles (210 km) to Little Rock, Arkansas. Almost everyone they encountered on their ride to Texas believed the men were on their way to fight in the Texas revolution. Crockett and his companions followed the Red River along the northern border with Texas and crossed into the state through Clarksville to Nacogdoches. Crockett loved what he saw in the Texas landscape. Immigrant groups had moved to the Tejas and Coahuila areas of Mexico, which would later make up much of Texas. While in Nacogdoches, Crockett learned that a Constitutional Convention was going to be held to make a formal announcement of independence for Texas and form a new republic. Crockett now told Texians he had indeed come to fight for them.

From Nacogdoches the foursome moved on to San Augustine, where Burgin and Tinkle decided to head back to Tennessee. In San Augustine, Crockett and William Patton made a pledge to swear their allegiance to the Provisional Government of Texas. On January 9, 1836, Crockett sent what would be his final correspondence to the family, writing:

> . . . I must say as to what I have seen of Texas it is the garden spot of the world the best land and the best prospect

for health I ever saw is here and I do believe it is a fortune to any man to come here[.] [T]here is a world of country to settle it is not required here to pay down for your League of Land[.] [E]very man is entitled to his head right of 4000-428 acres[.] [T]hey may make the money to pay for it off the Land.

I expect in all probability to settle on the Bodark or Choctaw Bayou of Red River that I have no doubt is the richest country in the world good Land and plenty of timber and the best springs and good mill streams good range clear water and ever appearance of good health and game plenty[.] It is in the pass where the Buffalo passes from the north to south and back twice a year and bees and honey plenty. I have a great hope of getting the agency to settle that country and I would be glad to see every friend I have settle there[.] It would be a fortune to them all I have taken the oath of the Government and have enrolled my name as a volunteer for six months and will set out for the Rio Grand in a few days with the volunteers from the United States all volunteers is entitled to a vote for a member of the convention or to be voted for and I have but little doubt of being elected a member to form a constitution for this Province.

SAN ANTONIO DE VALERO MISIÓN

When Crockett joined the Texian army, he had some personal reasons for doing so. It was an opportunity to acquire land as a reward for all those who served, and he was sure he would have a hand in writing the constitution for the new Texas Republic. Never one to shy away from a fight, Crockett was probably not thinking about the danger or his mortality. Others like Crockett were willing to fight the Mexicans, including pioneer James (Jim) Bowie and attorney William Barret Travis. Like Crockett, many of the men who came to

The Alamo, originally known as Misión San Antonio de Valero, was home to both Royalists and Revolutionaries during Mexico's 10-year struggle for independence. It became the site of one of the most famous battles in American history.

fight arrived from states as far away as Pennsylvania, New York, and Massachusetts, and countries across the ocean, including Ireland, Scotland, and Germany.

From San Augustine, about a dozen other men who joined up with Crockett and his nephew rode the rest of the way to the small, dusty town of San Antonio. Going on the ride to meet their destiny with Crockett were his cousin John Harris and friend Ben McCulloch. When they arrived in early February, they saw a frontier settlement built from the mighty oak and hickory trees whose stumps randomly dotted the dirt road. Most settlers were Mexicans, but there were descendents of settlers that had been there since the seventeenth century and a military presence, too. In fact, there had been a military presence in San Antonio for most of the 1800s. The Spanish had stationed a cavalry unit just across the San Antonio River in an aging building that had been a part of the town for almost 100 years. It was named Misión San Antonio de Valero or the Alamo (Spanish word for "cottonwood") in honor of the soldiers' hometown, Alamo de Parras, Coahuila, Mexico.

The Alamo was built as a religious mission in 1744 to use to convert Native Americans to Catholicism. The structure was not sound, and portions of the building collapsed by 1756. Though it was rebuilt, the mission began collapsing again, so the Church decided to turn the entire compound (about 4 acres or 1.6 hectares) over to the townspeople in 1793. The mission building continued to deteriorate but was later occupied by the Second Flying Company of San Carlos de Parras soldiers of the Spanish Army. Most of the soldiers in the company had come from Alamo de Parras. The Alamo remained occupied from 1803 to 1825. It would play a major role in the revolution and independence of Texas 10 years later.

9

THE SIEGE OF THE ALAMO

By 1835, tensions were high between American-born residents living in Texas and their Mexican-ruling authorities. American Texians wanted their independence, and Mexico's ruling dictator, General Antonio López de Santa Anna, wanted to keep Texas under Mexican control. Skirmishes between Mexican forces and American settlers had been occurring on and off since 1826, but the clashes escalated to larger attacks and counterattacks by 1835. In a battle that began in December 1835 between the 300 or so Texian and Tejano (Texans of Hispanic descent) volunteers and the Mexican troops quartered in the city, San Antonio became the final stand between the two warring factions. After several days of house-to-house fighting, the Mexican troops, led by General Marín Perfecto de Cós, were defeated. Cós's troops had retreated inside the Alamo but were forced to surrender when the volunteers had been assured of victory.

COLONEL NEILL'S ROLE

With General Cós's defeat, the volunteers took over the Alamo and moved inside. San Antonio was now under the command of

Colonel James Clinton Neill. Knowing the Mexican army would return to reclaim the city, Neill sent out a request for more military support to Sam Houston, a leader of the push for Texas independence. In *J.C. Neill: The Forgotten Alamo Commander,* writer Stephen L. Hardin shared Neill's plea to Houston:

> The men under my command have been in the field for the last four months. They are almost naked, and this day they were to have received pay for the first month of their last enlistment, and almost every one of them speaks of going home, and not less than twenty will leave tomorrow, and leave here only about eighty efficient men under my command. . . . We are in a torpid, defenseless condition, and have not and cannot get from the citizens here horses enough to send out a patrol or spy company. . . . I hope we will be reinforced in eight days, or we will be overrun by the enemy, but, if I have only 100 men, I will fight 1,000 as long as I can and then not surrender.

Though many accounts of what transpired next supports the belief that Houston sent orders to evacuate the Alamo and blow it up, that is not factually correct. Much of the blame for what happened at the siege of the Alamo has been placed on Colonel Neill, accusing him of disobeying orders and keeping the men at the fortress to face almost certain death or capture. In fact, Houston had requested permission from the governing council to order the evacuation.

Before Santa Anna and his troops converged on San Antonio, Neill had asked to be relieved of his duty to return home to attend to his ill family. He had not abandoned his duty out of cowardice. When Neill requested a 20-day leave, he asked William Barrett Travis to take command of the Alamo. It was Travis who had to ready Crockett and the 189 men for battle when he received word of Santa Anna's forces of 4,000 approaching the outskirts of the city.

Sam Houston

Samuel Houston, one of the most important figures in Texas history, was born on March 2, 1793, in Virginia. He came from a large family, the fifth of nine children (five brothers and three sisters) born to Samuel and Elizabeth. When his father died in 1807, the family moved to eastern Tennessee, establishing a farm near Maryville. Rebellious and angry, Houston ran away and lived among the Cherokee for three years.

(continues)

Sam Houston commanded the Texas army to victory over General Santa Anna.

(continued)

When war broke out with the British (War of 1812), Houston enlisted in the U.S. Army, eventually serving under Andrew Jackson. The two men became close allies, and Houston supported Jackson in his presidential bid. Houston served as a congressman from, and later as governor of, Tennessee, then moved to Texas, where he became an early supporter of independence for the state. He served as the first president of the Republic of Texas (1836 to 1846)—a sovereign nation created after Houston's troops defeated General Santa Anna and his Mexican forces at San Jacinto. When Texas gained statehood in 1846, Houston served as one of its senators in Congress. In 1859, Houston was elected the seventh governor of the Lone Star State. When the Civil War broke out and Texas seceded from the Union, Houston refused to support the Confederacy. Forced out of office, he moved his family to a rented home in Huntsville, Texas. Aging and fighting illness, Houston died on July 26, 1863.

BLOOD RED FLAG IS RAISED

On the morning of February 23, the sounds of oxcart wheels rolling over the ground awoke the men at the Alamo. Residents, with carts filled with whatever possessions would fit, were leaving town en mass. Soon the city of San Antonio would be empty of its Mexican occupants, who had been told by a messenger sent by Santa Anna the night before to leave. American civilians, who had gotten no warning and feared the danger ahead, fled to safety behind the walls of the Alamo as the Mexican army approached to take back the city.

When Santa Anna marched into town in midafternoon, he met no resistance and recaptured San Antonio without firing a single shot. All that was left to do was remove the Americans barricaded inside the Alamo. Preparing for Santa Anna's arrival, Colonel Travis ordered all of the walls and gates of the compound reinforced with whatever materials the men could find. When Santa Anna knew he was in viewing distance of the Alamo occupants, he ordered the raising of the blood-red flag that signaled he would take no prisoners. When Travis saw the flag, he ordered the firing of a single cannon shot in response. Santa Anna returned fire, lobbing several grenades at the fort.

When the boom of the artillery quieted, someone heard a bugle faintly sounding in the distance. Bowie thought perhaps the bugle was a call to meet and talk. Without consulting Travis, he scribbled a note in Spanish asking if a meeting had been requested and sent engineer Green Jameson out of the Alamo bearing a white flag. Santa Anna intended to recapture the fort and sent Jameson back with his own note. *Narrative* author Buddy Levy wrote,

> . . . the Mexican army cannot come to terms under any conditions with rebellious foreigners to whom there is no other recourse left, if they wish to save their lives, than to place themselves immediately at the disposal of the Supreme Government from whom alone they may expect clemency after some considerations [are taken up]. God and Liberty!

When Jameson returned with Santa Anna's reply, Travis knew neither he nor Bowie would be permitted to leave the Alamo under the honors of war and would probably be executed despite what the Mexican dictator said in his note. There would be no agreement. To let Santa Anna know his decision, Travis ordered another single blast fired from the cannon.

Santa Anna wasted no time in beginning his siege of the Alamo. The fortress was bombarded with cannon fire and gunshots well into the night. Mexican troops completely surrounded the compound. Inside, Crockett and the men tried to stay out of the line of fire. Bowie had become very ill and could not even participate in the fight. Travis knew he and the others were facing insurmountable odds of surviving the onslaught, but surrendering was not an option. The men would fight to defend an indefensible structure and would no doubt be overrun by the Mexican forces sooner rather than later.

The next morning amid rain and gray skies, the Mexican troops marched within 100 yards (90 m) of the southwest corner of the Alamo. Crockett and other sharpshooters headed to the wall and began exchanging fire for what seemed like hours. Though they brought down about a dozen of the enemy, a rush of other soldiers would just take their place. Skirmishes like this went on for several days as the men waited, praying that military reinforcements would arrive in time to make a real fight to hold off Santa Anna and his army.

One hope for help rested with Colonel James Fannin and his troops at Goliad. The intent was to leave Fort Defiance with 320 men and ride to San Antonio and engage the Mexican army from their rear flank. Unfortunately, the brigade did not get very far. Ill-equipped, poorly clothed and fed, and fighting fatigue in crossing the San Antonio River and muddy trails around it, Colonel Fannin soon abandoned the idea of reaching the Alamo in time. However, about 30 men from Gonzales Ranging Company of Mounted Volunteers managed to sneak into the fortress during the cover of night on March 1. Perhaps more importantly, Travis was unaware that Santa Anna and his army were moving closer to the garrison under that same cover of darkness.

Colonel Travis was grateful for any help he and the men could get, but he was puzzled by the lack of response from Sam Houston. It was probably better that Travis was unaware that Houston had been partying it up at the Constitutional Convention at Washington-on-the-Brazos (a Texas park where 59 Texians voted their declaration of independence from Mexico on March 2, 1836) while the survival of the men at the Alamo depended on help arriving in time. While the Texians were declaring their independence from Santa Anna's rule, the general resumed his shelling and bombardment of the Alamo. On March 3, the Mexican army put on a display of pageantry, military style. About 2,500 troops, dressed in their full cavalry attire, marched to music, drums, and weapons fire preparing to encircle the Alamo.

THE FALL OF THE ALAMO

With no hope of help arriving to fight off the enemy, Travis knew the Alamo would fall and Santa Anna would be victorious. For 12 days, the Mexican army let loose barrages of artillery fire, crumbling many of the old walls surrounding the San Antonio de Valero Misión. At dawn on March 6, Santa Anna roused his troops quietly from sleep to make a full assault on the Alamo. The Mexican general, rather than letting the Americans run out of ammunition and food, which undoubtedly would lead to surrender, was bent on making an example of those responsible for the rebellion. He would take no prisoners. Columns and columns of Mexican soldiers marched toward the Alamo. At 5:30 A.M., the sound of the call to battle blared from several buglers and the surprise attack was under way.

Most inside the Alamo were not prepared for the attack. Awakened and scrambling to their posts, the men were caught up in the frenzy of the moment. Adrenalin rushed through the men as they shook off the grogginess of sleep while trying to respond to the surge of Mexican soldiers approaching. Trying to get a handle on what was happening outside, Travis leaned over one of the cannon emplacements and saw a sea of soldiers climbing ladders scaling the walls of the outer fortress. Once the Alamo was breached, the Americans retreated to several of the buildings inside the fortress.

Crockett and several other men withdrew into the chapel. The Mexicans, far outnumbering their enemy inside the Alamo, began a room-to-room search, killing everyone they came upon. Some men fell from bullet fire; others died valiantly fighting in hand-to-hand combat, wielding knives and even swinging their rifles at the Mexican enemy. Few survived the overwhelming onslaught of the several thousand soldiers. The chapel held the only remaining defenders. After blowing the chapel open, the Mexicans surged forward to find six men inside, including Crockett.

For many years after the infamous battle at the Alamo, tales were told and written of Crockett's courageous fighting and death

Crockett (*standing with rifle raised in the air*) joined 188 men in defending the fort at the Alamo, and managed to hold off Mexican troops for nearly two weeks. Crockett was one of the last men standing after Mexican forces overran the Alamo. He and five other men continued to fight until they were surrounded and killed in the battle.

in battle. In truth, Crockett was captured and taken prisoner with the other five men in the chapel that day. Unwilling to kill the men in cold blood, General Manuel Fernández Castrillón brought them into an open area inside the mission walls. Santa Anna waved off Castrillón and ordered their immediate execution. In an instant, Crockett, frontiersman, hunter, woodsman, and politician, was dead. The deaths of the men at the Alamo were avenged a few months later by none other than Sam Houston. Named commander in chief of the Texas army, Houston led 900 men to the battle cry

A Legend Lives On:
Davy Crockett's Life After Death

Beginning in December 1954—more than 100 years after his death in 1836—the celebrated frontiersman became enormously popular with American children because of a five-part series on Walt Disney's TV program *Disneyland.* The episodes made a star out of Fess Parker, who portrayed Davy, and the show's theme, "The Ballad of Davy Crockett," sold millions of records. The series also generated two full-length movies: *Davy Crockett, King of the Wild Frontier* (1955) and *Davy Crockett and the River Pirates* (1956).

Kids could not get enough of Crockett gear, including books, toys, lunchboxes, clothing, camping equipment, and guitars. The most popular item was a replica of Davy's coonskin cap. *Time* magazine estimated in May 1955 that in the first three months after the TV series began, more than $100 million of Davy merchandise was sold. In all, $300 million of Davy Crockett gear—about $2 billion in 2008 dollars—would be snapped up by the time the craze ended. Even today, Davy Crockett continues to occupy a place in American history as a real-life legend. But why does he remain popular so many years after his death? The answer lies in the way he lived.

When Crockett died defending the Alamo, he was glorified as a courageous soldier, portrayed in depictions of the battle with his musket "Old Betsy," fending off Mexican soldiers with mighty blows. The truth was apparently not very different from that: Crockett kept up the morale of the defenders, according to a survivor, by playing his fiddle. Another survivor remembered Crockett as the "leading spirit" in the camp, supporting and advising military commanders William Travis and Jim Bowie. He was one of the last men standing after the Alamo fell. Along with just five other men, he continued to fight until they were surrounded, and Mexican general Antonio López de Santa Anna ordered the men executed.

(continues)

(continued)

Crockett's frontiersmanship was already legendary during his lifetime. James Kirke Paulding's popular 1831 play, *The Lion of the West*, depicted a character based on Crockett and helped popularize the backwoodsman legend. After his death, many of Crockett's colorful sayings were published in almanacs between 1835 and 1856.

By the late nineteenth century, Crockett's fame had begun to wane. But in the early 1940s, film producer, animator, and director Walt Disney expressed his belief that American history was "the story of progress animated by the triumph of ordinary citizens." He believed that larger-than-life heroes such as Johnny Appleseed, Paul Bunyan, and Davy Crockett should be better known by average Americans. "I think this is a good time to get acquainted with . . . the American breed of robust, cheerful, energetic, and representative folk heroes. . . . [T]hey are worth looking at—soberly and in fun—to re-educate our minds and our children's minds to the lusty new world called America."

"Remember the Alamo" and engaged Santa Anna and his weary forces at San Jacinto on April 21, 1836. During the battle, Mexican general Santa Anna was captured and taken prisoner.

News of Crockett's death took some time before it reached the East and his family. Because his demise had been reported on several other occasions during his adventurous life, family members hoped the news was premature. Eventually acceptance replaced hope, and they realized Crockett would not be riding up to the homestead smiling, having cheated death once again.

For a long time after his death, Crockett enjoyed a fame that included a television show and marketing of his famous buckskin outerwear and his coonskin cap. A statue of Crockett stands inside the Texas State History Museum, a park is named in his memory, and a tombstone marking his birthplace reads, simply, but appropriately: "Davy Crockett, Pioneer, Patriot, Soldier, Trapper,

Explorer, State Legislator, Congressman, Martyred at The Alamo. 1786–1836." Crockett may never have achieved the material success in life he always strove for, but he still enjoys the prominence in memory for his never-give-up attitude and his ever-hopeful view on life.

CHRONOLOGY

1786   Davy Crockett is born on August 17 in present-day Greene County, North Carolina. He is the fifth of nine children born to John and Rebecca Crockett.

1798   At age 12, Crockett becomes a "bound boy" and is hired out by his father to work for Jacob Siler on a cattle

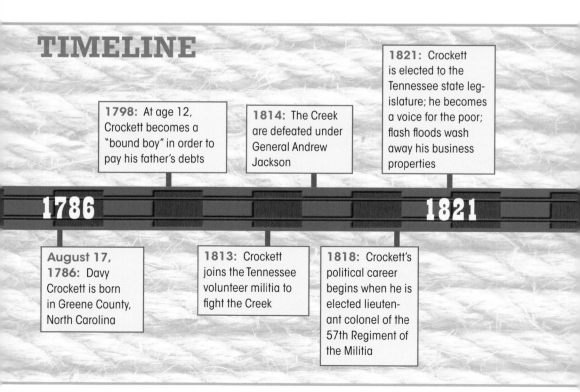

TIMELINE

1798: At age 12, Crockett becomes a "bound boy" in order to pay his father's debts

1814: The Creek are defeated under General Andrew Jackson

1821: Crockett is elected to the Tennessee state legislature; he becomes a voice for the poor; flash floods wash away his business properties

1786

1821

August 17, 1786: Davy Crockett is born in Greene County, North Carolina

1813: Crockett joins the Tennessee volunteer militia to fight the Creek

1818: Crockett's political career begins when he is elected lieutenant colonel of the 57th Regiment of the Militia

drive to Virginia. Siler tries to make him stay, but Crockett leaves with a band of passing wagoners.

1799   After a fight at school, Crockett runs away from home and does not return for two years.

1802   Crockett returns home at the age of 16.

1806   Crockett married Mary "Polly" Finley.

1807   Son John Wesley is born.

1809   Son William is born.

1812   Daughter Margaret is born.

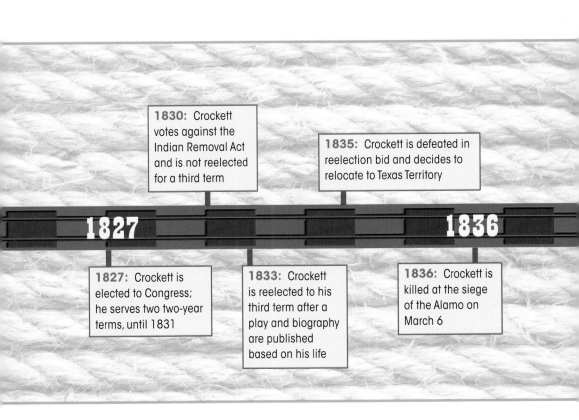

1830: Crockett votes against the Indian Removal Act and is not reelected for a third term

1835: Crockett is defeated in reelection bid and decides to relocate to Texas Territory

1827   **1836**

1827: Crockett is elected to Congress; he serves two two-year terms, until 1831

1833: Crockett is reelected to his third term after a play and biography are published based on his life

1836: Crockett is killed at the siege of the Alamo on March 6

1813   Crockett joins the Tennessee volunteer militia after the massacre at Fort Mims.

1814   As part of the War of 1812, Crockett fights the Creek tribe in Florida with the Tennessee Mounted Gun unit, serving under General Andrew Jackson.

1815   Wife Polly dies. Crockett marries widowed neighbor Elizabeth Patton, who has two children. Their first child, Robert, is born in 1816.

1817   While on a scouting mission, Crockett contracts malaria and almost dies. The family settles in Shoal Creek, in Lawrence County, Tennessee. On November 25, Crockett is elected the area's first justice of the peace.

1818   Daughter Elizabeth Jane is born. Crockett wins campaign to become lieutenant colonel of the 57th Regiment of the Militia. This election is the beginning of his political career.

1819   Daughter Rebeckah Elvira is born.

1820   By this time, Crockett owns 614 acres of land and a gristmill, a distillery, an iron-ore mine, and a gunpowder factory in Shoal Creek.

1821   Crockett runs and is elected to the Tennessee state legislature; he becomes a voice for the poor, a position he will uphold for his entire political career.

Daughter Matilda is born; flash floods wash away his business properties.

Crockett runs for Congress but is defeated in an ugly campaign by incumbent congressman

Adam Alexander. He later almost dies of hypothermia on a hunting trip.

1826   Crockett almost drowns in a boat on a business venture on the Mississippi River.

1827   Crockett is elected to Congress, where he serves two two-year terms until 1831.

1830   Crockett votes against President Andrew Jackson's Indian Removal Act and is not reelected for a third term to Congress.

1833   Crockett is recognized nationally by a play based on his life (*The Lion of the West*) and a book (*Life and Adventures of Colonel David Crockett of West Tennessee*). He moves ahead in the polls and narrowly defeats William Fitzgerald for a third term to Congress.

1835   Crockett is defeated in reelection bid and decides to relocate to Texas Territory.

1836   Crockett is killed at the siege of the Alamo on March 6.

GLOSSARY

consented   To give approval; agree

diplomacy   The ability to negotiate without stirring hostility

elated   To feel filled with joy or pride

encroach   To take another's possessions or rights gradually

furlough   A leave of absence from duty, especially for a soldier

germinate   To cause to sprout or develop; to begin to grow

hatter   One who makes, sells, or repairs hats

homesteader   A person who acquires or settles on undeveloped land by filing a record with the government and living on the land

hypothermia   A condition where the body's temperature is abnormally low from loss of body heat

immigrants   People who come to a country to become permanent residents

incumbent   Someone holding a specified office

militiamen   Members of a militia who are militarily trained and competent when called upon to serve

parody   An imitation, usually somewhat funny

primer   A small book for teaching children to read

rendezvous   To meet at an appointed place and time

respectable   Worthy of respect; fit of character and behavior

sharecropper   A farmer who works land for the owner in return for a share of the value of the crop

shenanigans   A funny or devious trick

sporadic   Something that occurs from time to time

unsavory   To behave badly

BIBLIOGRAPHY

Blaisdell, Robert. *Great Speeches by Native Americans.* Massachusetts: Courier Dover Publications, 2000.

Cobia, Manley F. Jr. *Journey into the Land of Trials: The Story of Davy Crockett's Expedition to the Alamo.* Franklin, Tenn.: Hillsboro Press, 2003.

———. *Davy Crockett, His Own Story: A Narrative of the Life of David Crockett of the State of Tennessee.* Bedford, Mass.: Applewood Books, 1993.

"David Crockett, Tennessean," Gibson County, Tennessee Biographies. Available online at http://files.usgwarchives.net/tn/gibson/bios/crkett01.txt.

Davy Crockett's Own Story as Written by Himself; the Autobiography of America's Great Folk Hero. Illustrated by Milton Glaser. New York: Citadel Press, 1955.

Groneman, William III. *David Crockett: Hero of the Common Man.* New York: Forge, 2005.

Heidler, David Stephen. *Encyclopedia of the War of 1812.* Annapolis, Md.: Naval Institute Press, 2004.

Jones, Randell. *In the Footsteps of Davy Crockett.* Winston-Salem, N.C.: John F. Blair, 2006.

Levy, Buddy. *American Legend: The Real-Life Adventures of David Crockett.* New York: G. P. Putnam's Sons, 2005.

Stanley, George Edward. *Davy Crockett: Frontier Legend.* New York: Sterling Publishing, 2008.

Sullivan, George. *Davy Crockett.* New York: Scholastic Reference, 2001.

FURTHER RESOURCES

Chermerka, William D. *The Davy Crockett Almanac and Book of Lists*. Austin, Tex.: Eakin Publications, 2000.

Krensky, Stephen, Debra Bandelin, and Bob Dacey. *Davy Crockett: A Life on the Frontier*. New York: Aladdin Paperbacks, 2004.

Sanford, William R. and Carl R. Green. *Davy Crockett, Defender of the Alamo*. Berkeley Heights, N.J.: Enslow Publishers, 1996.

Winders, Richard Bruce. *Davy Crockett: The Legend of the Wild Frontier*. New York: The Rosen Publishing Group, 2003.

Web Sites

The Alamo Official Web Site

http://www.thealamo.org/main.html

This official site for the Alamo has historical information about the Texas Revolution, the battle for the Alamo, and the major players involved. It also includes visitor information, lesson plans, and a newsletter, *The Alamo Messenger*.

The American Revolution—The Battle of Kings Mountain

http://www.theamericanrevolution.org/battles/bat_kmtn.asp

A comprehensive site with detailed information about the numerous battles fought during the American Revolution, including the Battle of Kings Mountain.

The Creek Indians of East Alabama

http://www.eastalabamaliving.com/pdf/creek_indians.pdf

This article about the Creek Indians relates the proud history of their existence in East Alabama.

Genealogy—Davy Crockett

http://joepayne.org/crockett.htm

The family tree of Davy Crockett, his ancestors, and his descendents.

The Hermitage—Home of President Andrew Jackson

http://www.thehermitage.com/

The former home of President Andrew Jackson, the Hermitage is now a museum that has seen more than 15 million visitors.

Muscogee (Creek) Nation

http://www.muscogeenation-nsn.gov/

This is the official Web site for the Muscogee (Creek) Nation, a tribal government located in east-central Oklahoma.

A Narrative of the Life of Davy Crockett: Internet Archive

http://www.archive.org/stream/narrativeoflifeo00croc/ narrativeoflifeo00croc_djvu.txt

The Internet Archive offers access to historical collections of works that exist in digital format. The site includes text, audio, moving images, software, and archived Web pages.

The Sam Houston Memorial Museum

http://www.shsu.edu/~smm_www/

The online location for the museum, dedicated to the life and times of Sam Houston. It includes a virtual tour, calendar and news listings, chronology about Houston's life, recipes, and photographs.

Texas State Historical Association—The Handbook of Texas Online/Houston

http://www.tshaonline.org/handbook/online/articles/HH/ fho73.html

This is the online version of the six-volume *Handbook of Texas*, plus 400 articles not included in the print edition. It includes information about Davy Crockett, Sam Houston, and other famous figures, places, and events that made Texas into the state it is today.

For More Information

The Alamo
P.O. Box 2599
San Antonio, TX 78299

Davy Crockett Birthplace State Park
1245 Davy Crockett Park Road
Limestone, TN 37681-5825

David Crockett State Park
P.O. Box 398
1400 W. Gaines
Lawrenceburg, TN 38464

PICTURE CREDITS

Page

INDEX

ABOUT THE AUTHOR

Judy L. Hasday, a native of Philadelphia, Pennsylvania, is a two-time graduate of Temple University, with a BA in communications and an EdM in educational media. Ms. Hasday has worked as a photo editor and freelance writer for more than 25 years. She is a published author of young adult nonfiction and has more than 25 books in print. She has won five book awards including three "Best Books for Teens" from the New York Public Library, a National Social Studies Council Book Award, and one from the Voice of Youth Advocacy (VOYA). Many of her photographs have been published in books and magazines, with her most recent publication appearing in the Travel Section of the *Philadelphia Inquirer*. Her photograph, which captured a calving moment of the Margerie Glacier, accompanied an article she wrote about cruising in Glacier Bay, Alaska. Ms. Hasday devotes much of her free time to providing her photography talents, volunteering to cover several nonprofit fundraising events for the Greater Delaware Valley Chapter of the Multiple Sclerosis Society and the Philadelphia Chapters of the National Ovarian Cancer Coalition and the Pancreatic Cancer Action Network. She enjoys the company of cat Sassy, parakeet Keats, and finches Brandy and Amari.